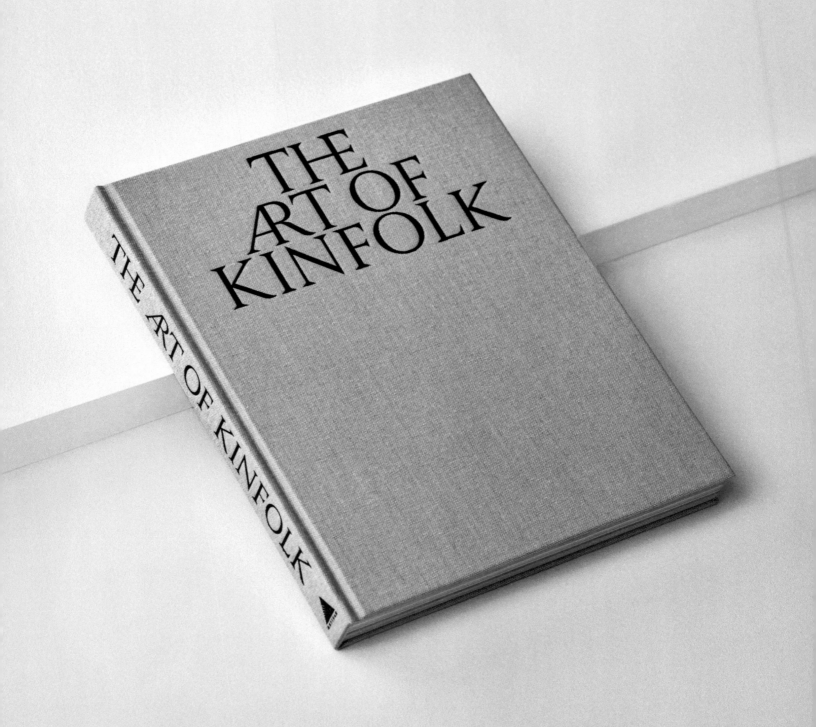

Play

KINFOLK

MAGAZINE
—

EDITOR IN CHIEF	John Burns
CONTENT EDITOR	George Upton
ART DIRECTOR	Mario Depicolzuane
DESIGN DIRECTOR	Alex Hunting
COPY EDITOR	Rachel Holzman

STUDIO
—

PUBLISHING DIRECTOR	Edward Mannering
STUDIO & PROJECT MANAGER	Susanne Buch Petersen
DESIGNER & ART DIRECTOR	Staffan Sundström
DIGITAL MANAGER	Cecilie Jegsen
ENGAGEMENT EDITOR	Rachel Ellison

—

CROSSWORD	Mark Halpin
PUBLICATION DESIGN	Alex Hunting Studio
COVER PHOTOGRAPH	Edgar Berg

WORDS
—

Precious Adesina
Allyssia Alleyne
Alex Anderson
Nana Biamah-Ofosu
Hannah Black
Wheeler Brown
Emily Chappell
Benjamin Dane
Daphnée Denis
Marah Eakin
Rowan El Shimi
Tom Faber
Thea Hawlin
Suyin Haynes
Elle Hunt
Robert Ito
Rosalind Jana
Tara Joshi
Jessica J. Lee
Francis Martin
Emily May
Emily Nathan
Okechukwu Nzelu
John Ovans
Carla Perez-Gallardo
Vera Sajrawi
Charles Shafaieh
George Upton
Alice Vincent
Annick Weber
Imogen West-Knights
Tom Whyman

STYLING, SET DESIGN,
HAIR & MAKEUP
—

Paloma Brytscha
Leonardo Chaparro
Roro Cuenca
Franziskus Dornhege
Victoria Granof
Sheldon Harris
Elise Jonke
Mindy Le Brock
Safiya Levers
Lee Levy
Christian Møller Andersen
Nicole Maguire
Lisa-Marie Powell
Julia Quante
Heather Rest
Sandy Suffield
Noriko Takayama
Michael Zumaya

ARTWORK &
PHOTOGRAPHY
—

Atelier Abraha Achermann
Nedda Afsari
Lauren Bamford
Edgar Berg
Edvinas Bruzas
Alexandra Cabral
Delfina Carmona
Rala Choi
Marina Denisova
Paw Gissel
Marco Galloway
Samar Hazboun
Max Hemphill
Iris Humm
Marley Hutchinson
George Kroustallis
Renée Kemps
Robin Kitchin
Cecilie Jegsen
Alixe Lay
Luke Lovell
Suleika Mueller
Cian Oba-Smith
Jessica Pettway
Makeda Sandford
Julien Sage
Søren Solkær
Joe Talbot
Aaron Tilley
Emma Trim
Priszcilla Varga
Sarah van Rij
Andreas von Einsiedel
Antonio Zazueta Olmos

PUBLISHER
—

Chul-Joon Park

Modern since 1949. Thousands of new combinations yet to be discovered.

WELCOME
The Community Issue

This winter, *Kinfolk* reaches a new milestone: our 50th issue. To celebrate, we're dedicating a special section to a theme that has been at the cornerstone of both our editorial coverage and our survival as a publication over the last decade —community.

It's an issue dedicated to fellow-feeling: Our contributors have fanned out across the globe to infiltrate small but inspiring groups who come together to connect, create, collaborate and care for one another.

"Community for me is where everybody can have the space and liberty to be who they are," artist and conservationist Vivien Sansour tells us on page 175. Sansour runs a seed bank in a small village outside of Bethlehem, where she works with local farmers to preserve heirloom seeds and, in turn, Palestine's cultural heritage for future generations. Her definition of community serves as a banner that guides the rest of the issue.

In California, for example, we meet the Old Gays—a group of gay elders whose later-in-life friendships and popularity on social media have made them curators of generational knowledge on a massive scale, and brought them tenderness and care as they party through their retirement. In the suburbs of Cairo, we visit the Ramses Wissa Wassef Art Center, a seminal piece of architecture and the home of several generations of women,

who have practiced traditional tapestry-making techniques from a young age. We join Velociposse—a group of women, trans and nonbinary people—for a leisurely cycle around London, and visit the oldest Quaker meeting house still in use, where people come together to worship in silence. "How often in your daily life do you get to sit down with a group of people and just be still?" one member asks.

Elsewhere, we meet people whose boundless creativity means they never quite stay still for very long. On page 48, musician Caroline Polachek speaks to Tara Joshi as she prepares to wind down from a two-year touring circuit, and on page 58, Annick Weber travels to the Provençal home of Benoît Rauzy and Anthony Watson, the inspiration for Atelier Vime and its revival of the traditional craft of wickerwork.

For this next chapter in *Kinfolk*'s history, we've added a slate of new columns that will recur in future issues, including seasonal guides to cooking, gardening and communing with nature, interesting jobs and the tools used to do them, and a dedicated space for leading literary lights. We hope you find it illuminating.

WORDS
JOHN BURNS

HOUSE OF FINN JUHL

The Chieftain Chair | Finn Juhl | 1949

The iconic Chieftain Chair is one of Finn Juhl's absolute masterpieces, representing the peak of his career as a furniture designer. At its introduction in 1949, the chair marked a renewal of the Danish furniture design tradition. Today, it is perceived as one of the most important exponents of the Danish Modern movement in the US during the 1950s. The chair is available in walnut or oak with upholstery in selected, exclusive leather types. Read more at finnjuhl.com

STARTERS
On whistling, walking and work.

FEATURES
A pop star and a perpetual stew.

"I see that people want to be a part of something. They want to be in on the joke." (Annie Rauwerda – P. 108)

COMMUNITY
Living, working, playing and praying.

DIRECTORY
New columns and old hands.

Photo: Paw Gissel

KINFOLK

NOTES

A new line of home and beauty products by *Kinfolk*, created to instil rituals and invite sensory pleasure into everyday life. Available at Kinfolk Dosan, Seoul.

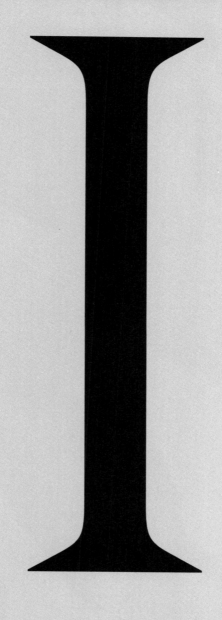

STARTERS
Tiny homes, boring museums and a recipe.

HELPING HANDS
How to volunteer.

So, you've decided to volunteer at your local soup kitchen. By all accounts, this should be a win-win. According to scores of studies, the mere act of volunteering—whether you're feeding the hungry, reading to old people or cleaning beaches—is the best sort of medicine. Volunteering has been shown to lower stress levels, reduce feelings of loneliness and make you feel better about the world and your place in it. And that's just how it helps *you*. There are also the people you're helping, the receivers of both your soup and your largesse.

Unfortunately, there are times when volunteering isn't purely positive. Voluntourism, which allows you to help out while on vacation, is perhaps the most problematic example. A typical project will see well-meaning voluntourists swoop down on a village in the Global South to build schoolhouses or pitch in at a medical clinic. Two weeks later, they return home, spiritually refreshed and with clear consciences.[1]

Most of these projects offer little more than quick fixes. In fact, it would be better if the voluntourists simply donated the money they would have spent traveling across the globe, enabling local laborers to build their own schools or clinics. Experienced residents would certainly be more successful than do-gooders who had never laid a brick before. And teachers and doctors will still be needed to staff those places—something that doesn't fit into the vacation plans of most voluntourists.

How can you ensure that your volunteering is making a positive impact? There are plenty of things to consider: Can you commit enough time and energy to make a worthwhile dent in the problem? This precludes most voluntourism projects, unless you have a lot of vacation days coming up.

Do you have any relevant skills? Most of us probably lack the experience to make a real difference when building youth centers or protecting rhino habitats.

And finally, do you feel strongly enough about the cause? Will you want to keep volunteering weeks or months down the line? There's always a chance your dedication will grow the more you volunteer, but it's also possible that you'll realize you don't care all that much about saving orangutans, and that you'd like to turn your attention to something easier and less jungle-y. Of course, there's nothing wrong with trying different things, but those who have dedicated their entire lives to their cause may not want to work alongside someone who flits from project to project.

Like anything else, you don't want to overdo it—sometimes people care so deeply about their volunteer work that everything else in their life suffers, and then they're no good to anybody. But you do want to pick a cause that you find valuable and worthwhile enough to sustain you through those times when the work doesn't feel very important or worthwhile. After all, many experts agree that it's not so much the nature of the activity that will keep you volunteering, but how meaningful the activity is to you, and how much you'd miss doing it if you stopped.

WORDS
ROBERT ITO
PHOTO
PAW GISSEL

(1) It has been argued that voluntourism implicitly teaches participants to develop a "white savior complex." In the words of a *New York Times* article, "simply by being privileged enough to travel the world" makes voluntourists assume that they "are somehow qualified to help ease the world's ills."

17

This simple recipe is a nod to the fundamentals of nourishment and necessity. When we have little, we make do and ensure the bellies of those we love are full. Stale bread can make a simple broth more filling and, in fact, if you look into the etymology of the word "soup," it originally meant "bread soaked in broth."

Our bread soup is a translation of an Ecuadorian recipe that sometimes calls for meat-based stock, but our version uses a humble mixture of milk and water. Make it when you need a warm hug or don't feel like making a trip to the grocery store.

(Serves 2)
2 tablespoons unsalted butter
1 tablespoon annatto seeds
1 bunch scallions, finely chopped
2 cups whole milk
Leaves from 3 sprigs of oregano
Kosher salt to taste
1 teaspoon freshly ground black pepper
½ cup crumbled queso fresco
1 day-old baguette, cut into
    1-inch-thick slices
Chopped cilantro, for garnish
Chile oil, for garnish

Melt the butter in a medium pot over medium heat. Add the annatto seeds and toast until the butter turns red-orange in color. Remove the seeds from the pot and discard. Set aside a small handful of the scallions for garnish, then add the rest to the pot and sauté until wilted, about 1 minute.

Add the milk, oregano, salt, pepper and 1 cup of water and bring to a simmer. Add the queso fresco, cover, and simmer over low heat for 5 minutes. Be careful not to boil the soup. Add the slices of day-old bread, stirring so they soak up the broth.

Divide among bowls, sprinkle with the cilantro and reserved scallions, and add a dash of chile oil.

—

This recipe is excerpted from *Please Wait to Be Tasted: The Lil' Deb's Oasis Cookbook*.

SOPA DE PAN
A Lil' Deb's Oasis recipe.

WORDS
CARLA PEREZ-GALLARDO
HANNAH BLACK
& WHEELER BROWN

As a kid, Molly Lewis was obsessed with learning to whistle. "I just really needed to make a sound with my mouth," she says, at ease on a sofa at home in LA one Tuesday morning. "It was a fun thing for me, and I was good at it." So good at it, in fact, that it's become her full-time gig. Since 2016, Lewis has worked with musicians as diverse as Mark Ronson, Dr. Dre and Kirin J Callinan, and released two EPs of her own. "I still pinch myself," she says.

ELLE HUNT: What makes a good whistler?

MOLLY LEWIS: People often ask me for whistle lessons, but I don't really know how to teach it. It's just about trying to form your mouth in many different ways. It's not one size fits all—you need to play around. I definitely have a talent for it, but I honed the skill over many years.

EH: Is there any crossover between being a good whistler and a good singer?

ML: I was never a good singer, but so much is about breath technique. The best whistlers can whistle while breathing in and out, so you don't have to stop to breathe—you can kind of go forever.

EH: What kind of work do you get?

ML: I moved to LA to study film. A friend in the art world asked me to perform at an opening, and I did a classical piece, then I met musicians who were interested in using whistling in some way. Every time I performed, something would lead out of it. It's slowly built into putting a band together, and a lounge show, and to making records and touring shows around the world. It's taken over my life, in a wonderful way.

EH: What is the strangest gig you've ever had?

ML: The director Alejandro Iñárritu had me overdub the whistling in his film *Bardo*. It's a recurring theme and he didn't think the actors were doing it well enough. He was directing me: "[The character] can't quite remember the tune, so do it a little unsure. And she's 80 years old." I don't think it ended up in the movie, but it was a hilarious day.

EH: What makes a good song to whistle?

ML: Opera is always great because it has these amazing leaps and dynamics. Old ballads are also good for that: You can really show off your range.

EH: How do you protect your instrument?

ML: I love lip balm, of all types. I have a huge range of Chapsticks. That's probably the only thing that a whistler can rely on. I definitely don't drink before a show. It's not good for your lip control. But as long as I can breathe, I can whistle. I heard of a whistler who wouldn't kiss his wife two weeks before a competition because he didn't want to bruise his lips. But that sounds like there was something else going on.

EH: Who would be your dream collaborator?

ML: I'd love to get into movie scores and collaborate with Tarantino, or else work with Abba. A whistle disco song—that would be success!

—

—

—

ODD JOBS
Molly Lewis, professional whistler.

WORDS
ELLE HUNT
PHOTO
ALEXANDRA CABRAL

PROMOTIONAL FEATURE

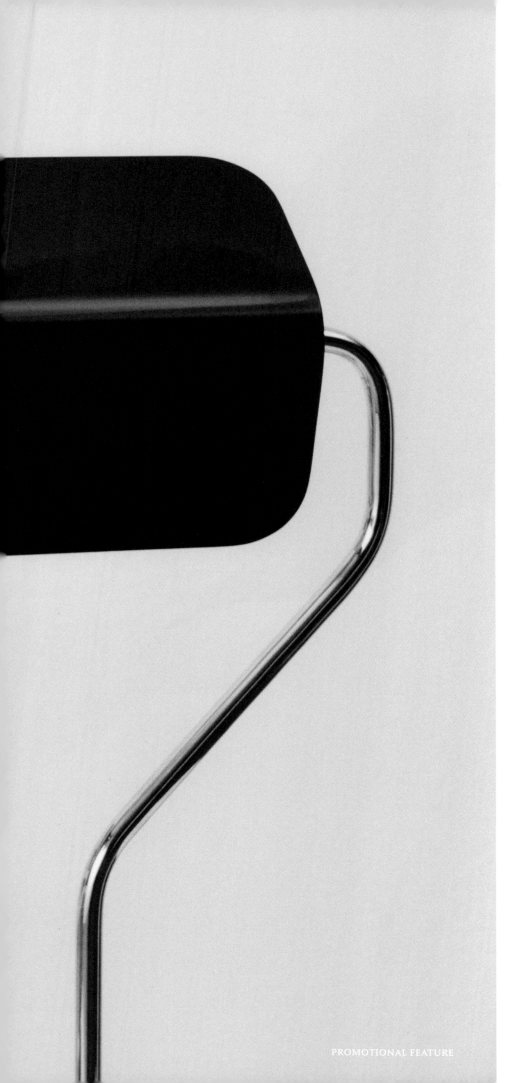

A hundred years ago, it was not uncommon to see accountants, journalists and those in other eye-straining occupations wearing green translucent visors to temper the harsh glare of early electric light bulbs. The Emeralite desk lamp, designed in 1909 by American engineer Harrison D. McFaddin, followed the same principles. Its green glass shade was thought to not only reduce eye fatigue and improve productivity, but to have a calming effect on employees. It was so popular with financial institutions that it came to be known as the "banker's lamp."

In part thanks to its ubiquity in movies—where it is used as a signifier of a certain established and learned authority—the banker's lamp has come to be a design icon. Now it is being reimagined by London-based designer John Tree for the Danish design brand HAY.

Tree's Apex series simplifies the form of the shade and introduces free-standing and clamp-on models. The folded steel shade creates a focused pool of light that echoes the purposeful intimacy of the banker's lamp. It is certainly unlikely to need the same revisions as its precursor, later versions of which were available with clocks, pen holders and even cigar ashtrays—anything to ensure auditors and editors stayed glued to their desks.

—

This post was produced in partnership with HAY.

WORDS
JOHN OVANS

MARIAM ISSOUFOU KAMARA

WORDS
NANA BIAMAH-OFOSU
PHOTOS
MAKEDA SANDFORD

Hair & Makeup: Safiya Levers

The architect building the ruins of the future.

Mariam Issoufou Kamara is a Nigerien architect and the principal of atelier masōmī, an architectural practice headquartered in Niamey, Niger. Her first major project—Niamey 2000, a housing scheme based on the traditional Nigerien compound house—was completed in 2014. Since then, Kamara has explored the traditional typologies, materials and building techniques of wherever her projects have taken her. These include the Hikma Community Complex, comprising a library and mosque, which won awards for sustainable architecture, and the Ellen Johnson Sirleaf Presidential Center for Women and Development in Liberia and the Bët-bi, a new museum and cultural center in Senegal for the Josef and Anni Albers Foundation—both of which are currently in development.

When we speak over Zoom, Kamara is in New York, where she's setting up a new design studio for atelier masōmī. As she explains, her architecture is rooted in memory and a love for history, but it is also resolutely contemporary and firmly situated in the present.

NANA BIAMAH-OFOSU: What was your earliest experience of architecture?

MARIAM ISSOUFOU KAMARA: I remember it quite vividly, but I didn't think of it in terms of architecture. It wasn't so much about form but a spatial and sensory experience. I grew up in the desert where temperatures were regularly between 45 and 50 degrees [113 and 122 F]. There was a covered area before you entered our house. Every time I came back from school, I couldn't wait to get there because it was so much cooler than outside. I'm convinced it's why I'm so obsessed with temperature in my architecture.

NBO: You started your career as a computer scientist. What brought you to architecture?

MIK: I wanted to be an architect before going into computer science, so arguably architecture was my earliest career choice. Archaeology was a close second. Growing up in the desert and visiting Neolithic sites, I realized the things in my history books were right outside my door and this fascinated me. This interest translated into the desire to become an architect, but I could not imagine pursuing architecture as a career. I didn't know anybody who was an architect, and it was never very clear what the path would be. I thought it would be better to do something more directly useful. This was in the late '90s, in the middle of the computer boom, so I went into computer science. I always regretted it. Later, my life experiences made me reflect on the spaces we inhabit, and I started seeing the role of architecture as a primary driver not only for colonization and erasure, but as a tool for reclamation. That realization, of architecture's direct usefulness in redefining ourselves, beyond the love of the subject as a craft, was what gave me the courage to study architecture—I felt that I was contributing usefully.

NBO: How did your first project, Niamey 2000, develop?

MIK: I was incredibly frustrated with this custom of making unsuitable Western homes in Africa. I always felt that these houses, designed for a nuclear family, felt diminutive and unequipped for the big lives we live in Africa. I became interested in exploring solutions that could better register how we lived and acknowledge how public space interacted with the interior of the home. I wanted to understand the different gradations of spaces I knew existed in our minds, but that our architecture did not yet manifest. It was interesting to see that the project we developed in response looked just like the traditional homes of southeastern Niger.[1] It meant that it was the correct solution.

NBO: Your way of working gives continuity to traditional knowledge systems. How do you work with masons, artisans and builders?

MIK: You have to find new forms of communication for working with builders in this context. Drawings are not always useful; we often use voice notes, images and sketches—sometimes literally sketching in the sand on-site. When we work with artisans, we're interested in understanding how they work, but I don't necessarily want to design buildings based solely on what they know. Stretching their existing skills is where the negotiation lies and that has often been the most exhilarating part of the process. I also approach every new context with a process of discovery, which sometimes confirms what I already know, or allows me to uncover something new. There's a certain amount of openness that's required, especially when you are trying to imagine new things that are very much anchored in old things.

NBO: You've previously spoken about the idea of the "echo"—the similarities between places, cultures and geographies. What places inspire the work you're making now?

MIK: Ultimately, it's about understanding that architecture gets its form from climate and geology. If I'm designing in Niger, I can learn from places like Rajasthan, where similar climatic conditions have led to interesting techniques for rainwater harvesting. Similarly, there might be a lot to learn from earth buildings in Tucson, Arizona. I'm less interested in geopolitical divides, like the Global North and South, and more driven by places that have an echo of my own context. It produces a more horizontal way of looking at architecture and a precedent where the global majority are in dialogue with one another and finding solutions based on our contexts.

NBO: I've read that you're interested in the idea of "ruin." You've said, "In Niger, we live in ruins." Can you explain what you mean?

MIK: It recently dawned on me that the common trait among buildings I really disliked was their inability to fall into ruin. It isn't necessarily because I prefer a certain type of materiality but rather because often these modern buildings, in steel, glass and concrete, just fall into decay. Ruin and decay are two separate things. The ancient architecture of parts of Africa and Asia exemplifies this idea—even in their fragments, they are still beautiful; they are ruins, they have not decayed. Why are we not making contemporary architecture in this way? Are we just making temporary skins to live in? If in the future someone were to excavate the architecture of today, they would think that we were all the same because our contemporary architecture all looks the same. I think that's a real pity.

NBO: You've described heritage as "inherited futures," which is interesting because it questions what it means to keep something alive. It puts the past and the future in the same time and space.

MIK: People often assume that I'm only interested in the past because of the way I talk about architecture. Actually, I'm obsessed with the future; I use the past to figure out what to make for the future. Unfortunately, in the 20th century, we decided that modernity required a tabula rasa—this has been an incredible waste of time and resources. It's why I'm passionate about the idea of the ruin in architecture. Ruins are the remnants of architecture that are the least harmful. Sustainable materials—earth, timber, stone—eventually go back to the earth. Gradually and slowly, they become beautiful ruins, whereas harmful materials decay, rust and pollute.

(1)   Many of the traditional homes in Zinder, Niger's third largest city, are built in the Hausa style, which is characteristic of the region. These typically comprise a series of rooms arranged around a courtyard.

26

CAPSULE WARDROBES
Unpicking a fashion staple.

WORDS
ROSALIND JANA
PHOTO
DELFINA CARMONA

Once upon a time in fashion land, you couldn't move for articles on the capsule wardrobe. Speaking in the language of *classics*, *staples*, *hero pieces* and *timeless investments*, they implored readers to think of their clothing as building materials. Good foundations, it seemed, were usually to be found in the form of the perfect white T-shirt, the perfect leather jacket, the perfect pair of jeans, the perfect knitwear and so on. There was a bland uniformity to these suggestions, a restrained reliance on elegant minimalism and trench coats fit for an Old Hollywood movie star.

The "capsule" wardrobe is largely understood to be a 1970s invention, with London boutique owner Susie Faux popularizing the term (although it's not clear whether it was her coinage or an earlier invention). It relies on the idea that, in a world awash with clothes, you can cut through the waves to reach something distilled, something essential. It exists in opposition to the fluctuations of tides and trends, providing a neat riposte to fashion's ever-capricious, ever-changing fancies. Designers such as Donna Karan soon capitalized on the idea, the designer's "Seven Easy Pieces" collection in 1985 cementing the idea that in order to get by, a well-dressed woman needed a base collection of garments including a wrap skirt, a bodysuit and some gold jewelry.[1]

Although it's not referred to with quite the same fervor today, there's still a good argument for the capsule wardrobe. Ideally, it offers a way of shopping and dressing that combines sustainability and longevity. At its most noble, it should make every purchase a special occasion: prioritizing things that will last for decades, providing a good base for the odd trendier item that brings a different kind of pleasure. Set against a backdrop of fast-paced, low-commitment consumption, it can slow the process down, making one more thoughtful about how money is spent and what it means to really love a garment.

However, while we might still see sweaters and jewelry as essentials, the fact that a Donna Karan wrap skirt wouldn't necessarily be top of one's "capsule wardrobe" list today points to a fundamental tension. Isn't timelessness itself a mutable concept? The capsule wardrobe of my adolescent *Vogue*-reading years had more than a touch of the off-duty-model-meets-Alexa-Chung-quirk that defined the era (think biker boots and Mulberry bags), while today's list might include tailoring of the-baggier-the-better variety: billowing trousers, blazers that drown shoulders. The garments that most of us are likely to own, such as jeans and sneakers, are better barometers of the time than a hemline: The fit and flare of the former and silhouette and sole of the latter are constantly being updated. Does the capsule wardrobe run the risk of accidentally becoming a time capsule, still trapped in the tastes of a particular age?

"Timeless" also tends to be equated with "expensive." A capsule wardrobe is much easier to create when one can afford high-quality knitwear or denim unpolluted by elastane. One could argue that it merely requires a mindset shift—a way of shopping that means buying a handful of things each year, for example—but that doesn't quite account for the capsule wardrobe's tendency toward aesthetic banality.

Perhaps the answer is to think less about capsules or classics, and more about what encapsulates a truly distinct approach to style. Some people look great in a perfect white button down paired with a perfect pair of black trousers. Some people look great in flamboyant dresses exploding with color and pattern. The truth is that *we* are the foundations of our wardrobes: our predilections and interests and desires, our continually honed understanding not just of what appeals and flatters, but what makes us feel good. It's only by digging down into our sartorial differences, rather than our similarities, that we can build anything truly lasting.

(1) Karan has continued to update and refine the Seven Easy Pieces collection over the years, to the extent that the designer once joked that her wardrobe should be called "seven easy trunks." The one constant piece has been the bodysuit.

WHAT ARE YOU WORKING ON?

WORDS
ROSALIND JANA
PHOTO
GEORGE KROUSTALLIS

David Koma's current workload.

David Koma's fashion designs are made for Really Dressing Up. Ritzy, risqué, silhouette-attentive—his high-octane pieces have amassed fans as big as Beyoncé. For Koma, however, it's all about the craft. For the most part, our Zoom call is made up of him showing me various garments on screen: "sorbet pink" fabrics, metallic bomber jackets, koi fish constructed from iridescent gems, and massed silk threads shivering like seaweed. These are clothes that demand attention, whether glittering on a stage or walking down the street.

ROSALIND JANA: Where do you work?

DAVID KOMA: My office is in east London, as is my apartment. It's a seven-minute walk from the office—my favorite timing, one cigarette away. It's also one street from the City: the whole juxtaposition of modern skyscrapers and this artistic world full of graffiti and culture. . . . Shoreditch has so much character. Our studio is in an interesting location—Shakespeare used to hang out here. I mean, I don't know how much I believe it, but they say that when he first wrote *Romeo and Juliet*, apparently he staged it here.

RJ: Do you ever feel his presence?

DK: In our courtyard, we have a sculpture of Shakespeare. . . . People often think someone is sitting there. Every morning, I say hello to him.

RJ: What's taking up your attention workwise at the moment?

DK: I'm still working on some custom |pieces|, based on a re-sort collection that was inspired by Aphrodite. Last summer, I went to my friend's wedding in Greece. I hadn't been there for a long, long time, and I took the opportunity to hang out in Athens. And just the spirit of the city and the amount of beautiful museums and sculptures and history and heritage |was so inspiring|. If you see the collection without knowing the concept, then it's beautiful on its own. But once you know where it's coming from, then you can start to imagine the different underwater movements and textures and tones.

RJ: How do you find the fashion world's pace?

DK: It's quite intense, but I'm the kind of person that always thinks if other people are managing to do it—and do it successfully—then I should be able to as well. I'm often asked how it's possible to have so many collections and inspirations, but after many years of working, I've developed my own system.

RJ: What part of your work brings the most pleasure?

DK: It's always a beautiful compliment when you see so many extremely successful women across different fields choosing to wear David Koma. I never get tired of it.

RJ: And what would you be doing if you weren't a fashion designer?

DK: I think I would still be in the art world, probably a sculptor or painter. . . . But if you would ask my parents, they would want me to become a tennis player.

Grooming: Roro Cuenca using Sam McKnight and NARS Cosmetics.

30

WORD: DUPE
On the next best thing.

WORDS
PRECIOUS ADESINA
PHOTO
PRISZCILLA VARGA

Etymology: The "dupe" is an invention of the internet. Back in the early 2000s, there were fewer high-quality beauty products and when they sold out, cosmetics enthusiasts would take to online forums to share alternatives or duplicates—"dupes" for short. By the time of the 2008 recession, however, "dupe" came to refer specifically to cheaper alternatives to sought-after brands. The term has since been popularized by money-conscious TikTok content creators (and is often spelled "doupe," "doup" or "doop" to reflect the exaggerated way the platform's users pronounce the word). Today, there are many influencers who have made finding dupes their life's mission, sometimes even when the shoe, bag, blow-dryer or lipstick they are duping was initially a dupe itself.[1]

Meaning: A dupe is an intentional or unintentional imitation of a coveted product, usually at a cheaper price point than the original. Dupe's place as an online trend initially found its foothold in frugality, especially among the beauty and fashion world, but it has since come to be an art in itself. Consequently, anything can be duped nowadays—from skin care and home decor to kitchen gadgets.

Beyond helping people save money, dupe culture celebrates a certain resourcefulness; it also prioritizes personal expression over status seeking and brand loyalty. Many dupes are as sought after as the original, and influencers have made successful careers by scouring the darkest corners of the internet—or at least taking a deep dive through Amazon—for them.

That said, many dupes are just knockoffs described in a less pejorative way. The term "has less negative emotional baggage than counterfeit or knockoff even though the word encapsulates counterfeit goods and products that look like other products," an intellectual property lawyer told *The Cut* writer Sangeeta Singh-Kurtz. But while copycats have long been associated with shady dealings and dishonest practices, the dupe celebrates transparency and authenticity, and consequently, in many cases, a popular dupe results in its original selling out, too. Some companies have learned to embrace the trend. In May, athleisure brand Lululemon held a "dupe swap" in Los Angeles where people could trade their duped leggings for the real thing. "We saw it as a really fun way to play into something that is a real part of our culture," Lululemon's chief brand officer Nikki Neuburger told CNN, adding that such an event allows the brand to "put the focus back on the original."

---

(1) In a reverse-dupe, in 2018, budget US shoe store Payless temporarily rebranded as "Palessi" and invited unwitting fashion influencers to a launch event in LA. Many attendees paid $600 for shoes that usually sell for $20.

It's only been an hour but you're tired. The Metropolitan Museum of Art has somehow become humdrum: Your neck hurts from craning to see beyond the crowds and, despite the famous objects on show, you're struggling to maintain a sense of wonder.

If this sounds familiar, then you've likely experienced museum fatigue. The term was coined by Benjamin Ives Gilman, the secretary of the Museum of Fine Arts, Boston, in *The Scientific Monthly* in 1916. Gilman blamed museum fatigue on the physical demands of inspecting artworks—peering into vitrines, reading the accompanying labels and walking between galleries. In 1985, a study in Florida showed that visitor interest peaked after around half an hour, and extensive research by museum exhibition consultant Beverly Serrell in the 1990s corroborated the idea that people had a limited time frame of interest.

In a world of ever-decreasing attention spans, is it any wonder that such vast collections of historical artifacts or priceless masterpieces can feel overwhelming? Objects deserve time and space, and often the traditional museum robs them of both. In one room, a single rusted arrowhead might draw a crowd, while in another gallery, a whole cabinet of them will only receive a cursory glance. It seems inevitable that we will need to rethink the museum, with natural human limits—both physical and mental—used as a guide for their design.

Research into mitigating the effects of museum fatigue cites variety as a defining factor. Variation in the type of objects, displays, lighting, and the incorporation of interactive experiences, can help visitors to feel in control. One study in 2018 also showed that visitors who made their own itinerary lasted longer than those who followed a suggested path. The solution to museum fatigue? It might simply be the freedom to follow your nose.

WORDS
THEA HAWLIN
PHOTO
RALA CHOI

MUSEUM FATIGUE
Bored? It's not your fault.

I WILL ALWAYS LOVE YOU
The enduring appeal of karaoke.

WORDS
OKECHUKWU NZELU
PHOTO
AARON TILLEY

You'd have a hard job pitching karaoke today, if it didn't already exist. Considered in isolation, the idea of performing in front of other people—especially strangers—is mortifying for most people. It's like public speaking, but worse: No one will really notice if you make an error in a presentation at work, but they will definitely spot it if you fluff the high notes on "I Wanna Dance with Somebody."

Despite this, karaoke-centered bars, video games and even wedding receptions abound. And there's James Corden's *Carpool Karaoke* for those who prefer their karaoke secondhand (with over three billion views on YouTube, it seems many do).

Strangely enough, lists of the most popular karaoke songs regularly feature tracks that would seem the most intimidating to untrained vocalists, either because they are musically complex, like Whitney Houston's hit, or because they are earnest and emotional, like *Billboard* magazine's most popular karaoke song, "...Baby One More Time" by Britney Spears. You might think that booze is behind all this—and it is hard to imagine karaoke being quite so popular without alcohol—but there's more to it.

According to Kevin Brown, author of *Karaoke Idols: Popular Music and the Performance of Identity*, karaoke is the ultimate leveler. "It allows all members of society equal access to a cultural space that is usually not available to the members of all classes," Brown explains.

It can, of course, be liberating to assume a persona, especially one that allows us to go outside our comfort zone, or experience a different way of moving through the world. But for many, karaoke is also about *performing the act of performing*, something between performance and play, tribute and mockery. We create these caricatures of stardom to insulate ourselves against embarrassment, and to make a safe, fun space for everyone, regardless of ability or confidence: Nobody expects greatness here. Above all, karaoke is a way to be comfortable with falling short of perfection—with a little help from our friends.

—

—

THE FAST LANE
Why speed is of the essence.

The way we walk has fascinated scientists for decades. Anyone who has seen a baby take its first steps knows how complex it is for humans to walk on two legs, even if most of us do it every day without thinking. As well as increasing our understanding of this feat of biomechanics, recent research has shown that the speed we walk can be indicative of certain lifestyle trends: Those who walk fast tend to live longer, for example, and are better able to recover after a stroke.[1]

We are all, however, walking faster than we used to: In 2007, academics at the University of Hertfordshire studied pedestrians in 34 cities around the world and found that the average walking rate had increased by 10% since the mid-'90s. Singaporeans were the speediest, managing 60 feet in 10.55 seconds, with walkers in Copenhagen, Berlin and New York in second, seventh and eighth place, respectively. The study hinted at why: The most dramatic increases in walking speeds were found in Asian cities, such as in Guangzhou in China, whose economies had been growing at a faster rate.

The study complements another finding—one that you may have observed yourself: People in cities have been found to walk faster than those in towns or villages. Time is money and the urban sprawl demands speed. If an impatient city-dweller is impeded by a bumpy sidewalk, they may well move to the street rather than slow down to navigate the cracks.

Evidently, walking speed is not only dictated by what we find most efficient or comfortable; there are other external factors at play. A 2018 study observed pedestrians in Seattle in the US and those in Mukono in Uganda to see how walking pace differed. Their findings highlighted differences between the two cultures: Walking pace slowed in Mukono when people were with their children, the better, it is assumed, to enjoy their company. In Seattle, pedestrians sped up with little ones in tow, perhaps because they had tasks to complete as a family.

The inverse was true for solo walkers: Those in Mukono were faster than lone pedestrians in Seattle, who seemed to slow down to savor their moment of solitude. So whether you prefer a leisurely stroll or a brisk march, there's no harm in walking a mile or two in someone else's shoes. After all, you might find they fit you better.

WORDS
ALICE VINCENT
PHOTO
SARAH VAN RIJ

(1) Fast or slow, walking has been key for many great thinkers. Virginia Woolf, Ludwig van Beethoven and Charles Darwin all used walking as an aid to inspiration, with the latter taking three 45-minute walks every day on his dedicated "thinking path."

35

CULT ROOMS
A modernist with the Midas touch.

WORDS
JOHN OVANS
PHOTO
ANDREAS VON EINSIEDEL

Ernö Goldfinger's first major project in the UK was 1-3 Willow Road in north London, built in 1938. The Hungarian-born Goldfinger had set out to create a home in Hampstead—where he and his wife had lived since 1934—that would showcase his talent as an architect, but the project was the subject of controversy rather than admiration at first. Though it is now one of London's best-known modernist homes, his plan involved demolishing a row of Victorian cottages, drawing the ire of local residents.[1] (According to some sources, this is why Ian Fleming named the villain in one of his James Bond novels after Goldfinger.)

The terrace of three red-brick houses (Goldfinger lived at the largest, number 2) took inspiration from the proportions of the surrounding Georgian architecture. The internal layout, however, was governed by Goldfinger's radical "hierarchy of space," where foldable partitions and changing floor heights, rather than corridors and hallways, allowed for flexible, open-plan living. With the exception of the external concrete pillars, and the concrete drum enclosing a spiral staircase designed by British engineer

Ove Arup, Goldfinger used natural, modest materials typical of socially conscious, interwar design. Much of the furniture and fittings—such as his desk, with its innovative pivoting drawers—Goldfinger designed himself.

Goldfinger lived at 2 Willow Road for nearly half a century, until his death in 1987, developing the ideas that would result in Brutalist residential high-rises like Trellick Tower, now a London landmark, as well as building a collection of art by Marcel Duchamp, Henry Moore and Max Ernst. Perhaps his greatest achievement, however, was doing all this despite the occasional prank calls from Bond fans, singing "Goldfinger!" down the phone to the tune of the 1964 movie's title song.

(1) In 1993, 2 Willow Road became one of the first modernist buildings acquired by the National Trust, the British heritage conservation society. Ironically, it was handed over by the heritage secretary, Peter Brooke, the son of Henry Brooke (the property's most vocal opponent during its construction).

38

HUMBLE ABODE
The appeal of tiny homes.

WORDS
ALEX ANDERSON
PHOTO
ATELIER ABRAHA ACHERMANN

The modernist designer Charlotte Perriand astounded critics when, just two years out of school, she exhibited a cramped interior entitled "Bar Beneath the Roof" at the annual fall exposition of interior design in Paris. It was a tiny room, lit by a single window under a low sloped ceiling. A nickel-plated bar and stools on one side balanced a built-in phonograph and leather couch on the other.

This was 1927, a time when young professionals like Perriand struggled to find decent housing in Paris. Yet virtually every other designer exhibiting in the show competed to outdo each other with grand rooms, exquisite finishes, lavish furniture and costly textiles. Art deco was in full swing, and Perriand was announcing a challenge—sowing "fruitful unease" among her co-exhibitors, as one critic put it.

Her creative use of spatial and financial constraints appealed to a small but influential group of modernists who were reshaping domestic spaces in Europe. Soon after the exhibit, Pierre Jeanneret and Le Corbusier hired Perriand to take charge of furniture design for their atelier, where many of her interiors developed a remarkably close and economical fit between furniture and space to accommodate modern ways of living.[1]

The phenomenologist Edward Casey describes this kind of close fit as an "attunement of the body in a place." We feel at ease in spaces well adapted to how we want to live. He explains that this is what gives us a powerful sense of being "at home." Very small spaces accentuate the possibilities for this, because every square inch calls out for the designer's creativity, pushing them to develop ingenious ways of blending the functions of rooms, furniture and storage.

Recently, environmental and social imperatives have reinforced the value of this spatial economy. Small, well-designed dwellings make sense for big reasons. Never Too Small, an Australian media firm that highlights what they call "Small Footprint Living" proposes that through good design of small, sustainable living spaces, "we can transform the way we live and interact with our growing cities; tackling urban overcrowding issues globally whilst improving the quality of life."

Many of the designs featured by Never Too Small demonstrate how small spaces offer this close fit by being flexible: A wall swings open to uncover a well-equipped kitchen; another slides to hide a bookshelf and storage. This kind of alignment not only accommodates a range of needs but also engages people in the configuration of their own living spaces.

There is something deeply appealing about these clever mechanisms, as they transform cramped spaces into homes that fit the reality of people's daily lives. But tiny living spaces, cunning as they might be, place their own demands. People must constantly enact their spatial transformations (bedroom becomes living room becomes bedroom...); they need to shop frequently to make up for limited storage, and venture into the city to stretch out. These actions decisively transform the way people live and how they interact with cities. But as Perriand showed nearly a century ago, the fruitful unease that comes with new ways of shaping space can lead to vast new possibilities for contemporary living.

(1) For those who like their homes even tinier, many design brands have released miniature versions of classic pieces, including several by Charlotte Perriand and Arne Jacobsen. Just don't expect the prices to be quite so tiny.

BEIGE FLAGS
Dullness be damned.

WORDS
MARAH EAKIN
PHOTO
CECILIE JEGSEN

What exactly is a #beigeflag? The term was originally coined by an Australian woman in 2022 to refer to the traits people commonly list on dating profiles but that reveal very little about who they actually are. (Examples include liking travel, being a fan of *The Office* and preferring dogs over cats.)

Since then, the term has become one of the hottest trends on TikTok, accumulating over a billion views. In the process, it has evolved to describe a trait in a partner that's neither good nor bad, just a bit weird or boring. These idiosyncratic quirks can be as mundane as setting timers instead of alarms, or having to keep the coffee mugs in the kitchen in a certain order. Others are slightly less anodyne, such a boyfriend's predilection for eating ants he finds around the house, or a partner's "scary ability to gaslight." The latter would perhaps more accurately be described as a red flag—the term, which denotes unhealthy or manipulative behavior, from which beige flags derive.[1]

Compared to red flags, we all have beige flags in spades. Being in a relationship with someone is saying you're committed to who they are as a whole, oddities and all. Having some minor idiosyncrasies doesn't make someone undateable. It makes them an interesting, well-rounded person—provided that those little quirks are innocuous enough that you'll either be able to accept or learn to love them. That can change with time, too—a beige flag about a partner's seemingly benign obsession with Lego can turn bright red when you discover they've remortgaged the house to fund their hobby.

The age of social media and online dating has made many feel that they have to simultaneously seek out and model perfection—or at least value a blandly acceptable eccentricity. After all, the act of sharing your partner's beige flag online is loaded with subtext—a humblebrag that's calculated to reveal your sweetheart's most palatable quirk, and your gracious tolerance of it, without acknowledging the inevitable ups and downs of your relationship. It also offers a glimpse at how willing you are to share intimate details about your relationships to court favor online. Now that's a beige flag if ever there was one.

(1) There is a spectrum of color-coded flags to help people sort through the chaos of modern dating. However, out of nine different flags only two are indicative of positive relationships. Perhaps unsurprisingly, these are green and white.

41

SALLY POTTER

WORDS
CHARLES SHAFAIEH
PHOTO
ANTONIO ZAZUETA OLMOS

The film maestro on her musical debut.

Since the release of Sally Potter's first feature film, *The Gold Diggers*, in 1983, commentators have obsessed over her experiences as a female filmmaker. The acclaimed writer and director of *Orlando* and *Ginger & Rosa*—and over a dozen other films—finds this fixation exasperating. "Don't you want to talk about how I work with light and actors, about structure and narrative, about illusion, transcendence and all these fantastically interesting things that make up cinema?" she says, recalling these exchanges. Potter defines herself, rather, by what she makes—and that includes music. Following stints in bands such as the Feminist Improvising Group and composing scores for many of her films, she released her debut studio album, *Pink Bikini*, in the summer of 2023. The intimate, semi-autobiographical record gives a snapshot of teenage life in 1960s London and reconfirms Potter as a constantly inventive artist unsatisfied with restricting herself to a single art form.

CHARLES SHAFAIEH: Was the directness of *Pink Bikini*, in the lyrics and its conversational tone, intentional?

SALLY POTTER: Absolutely. This was about choosing a plain, raw vocal sound, as if I'm singing to just one other person. That's the principle with which I work on films, too. It's an illusion that you're making a film for millions. You have to direct as if for your dearest friend. I don't need to overdramatize, but I do need to be truthful. Every stage—from choosing the type of microphone to the mastering—had a discussion about intimacy and purity of sound.

CS: Your films also utilize direct address frequently, but often nothing is what it seems. Clarity and the mysterious coexist.

SP: I'm very interested in mystery but not in mystification. False mystery is when the filmmaker or writer is willfully holding back a piece of information to create puzzlement. When you're being raw and open, what becomes evoked is the greater mystery: Who the hell are we? What are we doing here? How do we relate to each other?

CS: *Pink Bikini* touches on subjects few people sing about today, such as banning the atomic bomb. Other songs engage with topics like teenage sexuality in a more frank—even taboo—manner than is typical.

SP: Because they're true. It's really simple: I remember during my teenage years the longing that was erotic, that was love, and the confusion of whether I wanted this or that person—the passions I had for other girls in friendship and in love, and for boys who I thought were so desirable I could die. I suspect that level of passion and desire is present through most people's teenage years, but they hide it away.

CS: There's a difference between sensationalism and honesty.

SP: Quite honestly, sexuality in films makes me want to throw up. Explicitness, in a funny way, hides real feeling. It loses contact with desire as a vulnerable and delicate, albeit also strong and powerful, thing. Sensationalism numbs everyone and turns everything into a performance. My criterion for that kind of writing on this album was to be vulnerable and true, but not to do anything for effect.

CS: Is that why none of the songs are sentimental? Rebellion and action—recurring themes on the album—don't allow for that.

SP: I'm not a fan of sentimentality, but I'm a great fan of sentiment —of true feeling and true thought. We are thinking-feeling-body-mind creatures. Sentimentality is when it becomes fake.

CS: In your films, people are often depicted listening—to records, city sounds, others having sex. The music is frequently heard by the characters too. Is sound often overlooked in films?

SP: Looking dominates people's experience [of cinema]. There's this huge image which is so full of information that, to absorb it, you're scanning and scanning, and your brain is processing the clues the filmmaker gives about the character, their life, their environment. A lot of people absorb the sound subliminally. I've always been interested in working with sound in a much more conscious way. I compose tracks or the whole soundtrack; I curate music from other musicians as well as silence, which has sound. You start to tune the sound effects, too. As far as I'm concerned, it's all music. The word "listening" is very important to me. It takes one person listening to change the dynamic in any conflict. I always talk to actors about not just being "on" when you're speaking—you're "on" when you're listening. The most interesting character on screen is the one listening to the other one. An awareness of listening as an active, not passive, state is crucial.

44

CHARM OFFENSIVE
In praise of ugly urbanism.

WORDS
TOM WHYMAN
PHOTO
MARLEY HUTCHINSON

What do we really mean when we call something "ugly"? We tend to use the word to describe something that is somehow unappealing. Of course, there are plenty of ugly things: an ill-fitting suit, a drab new office building, a shopping cart dumped in a river. But when things are unpleasant because they're ugly, it's usually because they're also boring or harmful; because they make us, and our environment, worse. This sort of "ugliness" is purely negative.

But just think of all the many wonderful things a different sort of ugliness—a more determined, more creative, more *positive* ugliness—can achieve.[1] From the grotesque and comic fusions of medieval marginalia, to the indignities perpetuated on the body in the paintings of Francis Bacon, and the auto-tuned frenzy of experimental musicians 100 gecs: "Ugly" things work not just against but with the beautiful; expanding and transforming the way we see the world.

Indeed, I would go so far as to argue that this positive ugliness is necessary for living well. Who, after all, would want to live in a "perfect" world? Think of something like Vermeer's famous *View of Delft*, a painting that is about as close to a representation of an ideal cityscape as one could ever hope to see. Vermeer's work is exquisite, but it is also terrifying: a piece of urban taxidermy, dead and fixed forever in the 17th century; the city painted from the far bank of the river and devoid of life. To me, its message is clear: The perfectly beautiful city, the city without flaws, would be fit only for the gods.

After all, what makes a place feel like a home, if not its imperfections? I feel at home when I see the dilapidated signs of the grocery stores in my neighborhood, where the people behind the counter always ask after my kids; when I see front gardens that have grown feral, teeming with mint or strawberry plants; when I see junk scattered in the road—some of which might be salvaged to fix something around my apartment, or else just serve as an ornament.

Without ugliness, without imperfection, beauty spins frictionless; it gains no purchase on the world. Real, unabashed ugliness should be celebrated. One aspires to be beautiful, and one desires lovely things. But ugliness is the stuff of life.

(1) In his 2007 essay *On Ugliness*, Umberto Eco wrote that: "Beauty is, in some ways, boring. Even if its concept changes throughout the ages... a beautiful object must always follow certain rules... ugliness is unpredictable and offers an infinite range of possibilities."

WORDS
IMOGEN WEST-KNIGHTS
PHOTO
LAUREN BAMFORD

House-sharing gets harder as you get older. The pool of people you can stand to live with shrinks as your friends start to couple up and move in together. You have a better idea of how you want to live, but you also realize that not everyone can give that to you, and you have far less energy for when disputes inevitably occur.

There are however some things you can try in order to achieve domestic peace. The first is to get a cat. A pet gives even the most fractious housemates something to agree on: Your pet is the most beautiful and perfect creature on earth. It may be hard to believe now, but you will naturally come to feel this way about your own future feline.

Everyone has different levels of mess they can tolerate. A truly filthy housemate is not a viable prospect in your 30s, but differences in cleanliness can be overcome providing you have one key housemate: the rare person who is willing to call out bad behavior quickly and with good cheer. Seek out this special individual and cherish them. And aim for a minimum of one bathroom per two people.

A common plague of shared houses is the passive-aggressive note. These notes do sometimes need to be left, but it's good to find a way to leave messages for your housemates that do not become rants about separating the recycling. One way to achieve this is to tally your Ws and Ls. This can be done on a whiteboard stuck to the fridge with sections for each housemate where you can write in "wins" and "losses." At the end of the week, count them up, and the whole house either wins or loses that week. It's a nice way to catch up, tease and celebrate each other, as well as being a good outlet for vacuous sentiments such as "W: Cat is so soft."

Final suggestions: Do not economize on your vacuum cleaner; save time by communicating through house emails instead of house meetings; and from extensive anecdotal evidence, do not live with anyone in their 30s whose main pursuit in life is "DJ."

HOW TO HAVE HOUSEMATES
New rules for communal living.

FEATURES
From LA, Barcelona and Provence.

Words
TARA JOSHI

Caroline POLACHEK:

TE SLOW BURN SUPERSTÆR.

Photos
NEDDA AFSARI
Styling
MINDY LE BROCK

"I learned to have very little faith in the music industry."

(above)   Polachek wears a vintage T-shirt by REPLIKA VINTAGE and a vintage ANN DEMEULEMEESTER scarf.
(previous) She wears a top and skirt by CARVEN.

FEATURES

Caroline Polachek is careful about what she gives away. "I think we're taught to not be mysterious," says the 38-year-old singer, songwriter and producer. She's reflecting on her experience in the music industry but you'd be forgiven for thinking she was talking generally about life in the social media age. "We're taught to reveal everything, to do behind the scenes, then do behind the scenes *of* the behind the scenes."

Polachek is speaking via video call from her London apartment, the sunlight catching on the bleached part of her dark brown hair. Though she is affable and erudite when discussing her career, the Connecticut-raised artist seems most comfortable steering the conversation down tangents that allow her to open up while still being mindful of what she's sharing.

"I really try to make an effort to hang on to my early impulses toward mystery and all the magic that is contained in the craft of things," she continues, sharing a piece of advice learned over her long, successful career: "Once you've taken the time to create [something], don't undo it. Don't undo it by overstating your case; let it be what it has aspired to be."

It's a mindset you can hear in her work, notably in the two sleek, beautiful albums she released under her own name: 2019's *Pang*, and 2023's *Desire, I Want to Turn Into You*. Both invite listeners into expansive, chaotic worlds that do not conform to typical pop-music tropes or themes. The production is rich and complex—the latest album, which ranks as one of the best records of the year,[1] features bagpipes, "itchy and primitive" drums, warm bass and choirs of children—but it's Polachek's voice that makes these records astonishing. She flits between quasi-cyborg Sprechgesang (a combination of speaking and singing), mellifluous pop and an operatic howl. If you catch her live, there is a collective joy and hilarity in attempting to sing along with what she calls her "hyper-expressive vocals."

For Polachek, just hearing her voice take center stage can feel like she's revealing too much. "The thing that eats at me a little bit is how subjective my music is." She adds, "It's very main-character-y, you can't get away from 'Caroline Polachek,' and sometimes I do have these longings to make more instrumental music or less narrative music; music that allows the listener more space to project into rather than being so beholden to what I'm saying."[2]

For now, though, she accepts her current sound. "I can't really help but make songs in that way, [and] that have a lot of heart, and really describe myself," she says, adding with a laugh, "even if I'm sick of myself."

Polachek was hardly an unknown entity when *Pang* was released and her trajectory has been well-documented: In 2005, while attending the University of Colorado, she formed the indie synth-pop group Chairlift with her friend Aaron Pfenning; they put out three

---

(1)   *Desire, I Want to Turn Into You* received an average score of 94 on *Metacritic*, which assigns a rating out of 100 to reviews from mainstream critics. Polachek's score indicates "universal acclaim."

(2)   Polachek released an instrumental music album, *Drawing the Target Around the Arrow*, in 2017 under the moniker CEP—her initials.

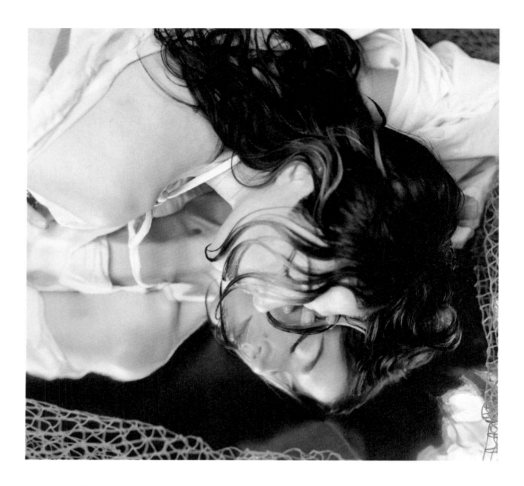

records between 2008 and 2017 (their song "Bruises" was famous-ly used on an iPod Nano commercial). She also released two solo albums in 2014 and 2017—via the monikers Ramona Lisa and CEP, respectively—but the first record under her own name brought a marked shift to a more personal, more intimate approach.

"I think I learned to have very little faith in the music industry with Chairlift," she says. "And not just the label system, but also music journalism. Because we were based in Brooklyn, we were 'making indie rock,' and by our third album we were absolutely not making indie rock."

Being signed to a major label, she also experienced the shift in the industry toward a more data-based approach, fueled by social media metrics and streaming figures. "Suddenly A&R was based on stats, not a perception of trends or what a good song was supposed to be. All of it completely dissolved my faith in these institutions... which was kind of perfect."

Polachek released her two most recent albums on her own label, Perpetual Novice, and she seems more grounded in her career these days because of it. "I'm willing to take a financial risk on myself be-cause I believe in it," she explains. "I will communicate [my ideas] with more depth, and not subconsciously rely on a team around me to convey the beauty and importance of these things. I think feeling

(above)   Polachek wears vintage pieces from the stylist's archive.
(previous) She wears a top and skirt by CARVEN.

that I was on my own, and that I was financially on the line for all my own decisions, is really a big reason for why this solo project ultimately found its feet."

Exploring the jarring contradiction of being both a new artist and an established one, she says she was afforded the "indulgence of a clean slate" with the release of *Pang*. Initially, she felt her fan base fell into two distinct groups—the indie Chairlift fans who had stuck with her, and the newer PC Music fans (many of her collaborators as a solo artist are from the eclectic London-based label).[3] Now that her second album is out in the world—made in partnership with Danny L Harle of PC Music—Polachek thinks her fan base feels "much more mysterious and exciting." At the shows, she sees "multiple cultures happening at once: the more serious listening culture, the girls in their bedrooms writing their dissertations and crocheting, the people actively and very creatively interfacing [by] making fan art, making edits, being active on Reddit and Discord, and then... you know, the people who are just on Twitter."

It's an ever-growing group of listeners, not least because of Polachek's time on the road, sharing her music with new audiences. When we speak, she is coming to the end of two years of almost nonstop touring—midway through our call, she has to pause because a courier arrived to pick up the last of her festival circuit wardrobe. It concludes a cycle that saw her supporting Dua Lipa on the US leg of the Future Nostalgia tour, collaborating with Charli XCX and Christine and the Queens on the glorious "New Shapes" and, of course, releasing the highly acclaimed *Desire, I Want to Turn Into You*. She says the tour helped her express the record in a new way, and made her more aware of its physicality and intensity. "I'm sort of figuring out how to be a normal person again," she says, reflecting on it all.

When she does get some downtime, Polachek likes to spend it in nature. It's a dominant theme in her work; in *Desire, I Want to Turn Into You*—both in the lyrics and in the music videos—there are lush vineyards, undulating blue oceans, ants crawling in sheets and, perhaps most notably, reference to volcanoes, ashes, dust, the cracked earth. She sees it as an acknowledgment of "a sort of faceless, chaotic vitality, and also societal breakdown and personal regeneration, looking at the textures of things that feel ambiguously ancient [...] keeping things feeling always very physical and a little gnarly."

She explains that this is in part a response to feeling that people have lost touch with nature. "We've protected ourselves from it with technology [and] what's left of our relationship with natural symbolism is so deep in our unconscious [...] the nonhuman world, we're not privy to it," she says. "The landscape of the soul and human desire is the new environment." Accordingly, she uses her art to explore the contrast between the natural world and the egotism

(3)   PC Music is a loose collective of songwriters, producers and singers known for creating pitched-up pop music. Its founder, AG Cook, produced Polachek's songs "Ocean of Tears" and "Hey Big Eyes."

of human melodrama, poking fun at what she describes as her own "stupidity" and "narcissism."

Polachek recalls listening to Radiohead as a teenager and feeling that "they had created an aesthetic set of answers to being lost in the world." She hopes her own work will have the same effect, becoming an oblique form of communion between Polachek and her listeners. "It's interesting because it almost becomes a form of shield, this music becomes a barrier that answers a lot of these questions for you as a listener. That's what makes it art, not just music; it's grappling with bigger questions, rather than just 'How do we make your ears feel good?'"

She says she's been reflecting on a story she heard about Miles Davis from her tour drummer, Russell Holzman, whose father played with the legendary jazz musician. "Someone asked Miles, 'What's the thing you're best at?' and Miles thinks about it for a second and responds, 'Knowing who to pick.' Rather than saying he's a great musician or a great trumpet player or whatever, he's a great curator—and I think you see that with everyone from Kanye West to Beyoncé, knowing who to pick.[4] I really felt that transform my life for the last seven years, being surrounded by incredible musicians who I also felt this deep kinship with on the road."

In much the same way, Polachek seems to have found a balance between a desire for mystery and magic in her work and the need to open up to connect and collaborate with the people around her.

"I think in this world where we're taught that everyone is an artist with a capital 'A' and everyone is an island with a capital 'I'. That's not exactly how it works." Through her music—chaotic, self-satirizing and almost instinctively beautiful—Caroline Polachek is going some way to remedy this.

(4)   Beyoncé asked Polachek to produce several tracks for her self-titled fifth album including "No Angel," which made the final cut.

ATELIER VIME

Inside the Provençal home that inspired a craft revival.
Words ANNICK WEBER
Photos MARINA DENISOVA

It's late afternoon and Benoît Rauzy and Anthony Watson's dog, Alma, is sleeping peacefully in a corner of their Provençal home, her ears occasionally twitching in response to the birdsong in the garden. Sunlight is flooding through a set of French windows, casting a warm glow over the arabesque-patterned floor tiles and the room's yellow lime-washed walls. An 18th-century Aubusson tapestry glows golden as if illuminated from within. The scene has a painterly quality: It's not for nothing that the South of France—a land of sun-baked colors and fierce light—has fired the imagination of generations of artists.

We're in the "summer salon," so named for its sunny exposition and color palette. There's also a snow-white-walled "winter salon" on the other side of the house, but it's in this cheerful room that the three spend a

lot of their time, no matter the season. "In the summer, we have the shutters closed to keep the room cool; in the winter, there's a fire to warm it up," says Rauzy, taking a sip from his coffee before placing it on a low rattan table in front of him. "We live in all the spaces of the house all year round."

Anyone familiar with Rauzy and Watson's design firm, Atelier Vime, will have seen pictures of the couple's gray-shuttered *hôtel particulier* and its dozen or so rooms on the studio's social media feed. For in addition to being a comfortable family home, the house is also the backdrop against which Rauzy and Waston photograph the pieces from Atelier Vime's collection of wicker, cord and rattan furnishings, with each shot resembling a tableau of bucolic Provençal living.

When the couple bought their then-crumbling mansion in Vallabrègues, a sleepy

village sandwiched between Avignon and Arles, in 2014, they didn't know it would become the heart of a new business. Rauzy and Watson—an environmental consultant and stylist, respectively—had originally sought a retreat from their busy lives in Paris, but upon renovating the property, they uncovered a piece of local history that they resolved to save from oblivion.

Scattered around the house were hundreds of woven baskets, revealing the property's past life as a 19th-century wicker workshop in what was once a thriving basketry town. As they settled in, Rauzy and Watson decided to establish a studio for handwoven home accessories and antiques in the same space. "Atelier Vime is born of this very house and village. It wouldn't exist had we not moved here," says Rauzy. "Our home is our aesthetic universe," adds

Watson, as he points at the ceramic pots and oil paintings sitting atop a limestone fireplace. "If a piece works well in this setting, we know that it's worthy of the Atelier Vime stamp."

The three floors of their home showcase the couple's typical aesthetic mélange of Louis XV chairs, Directoire candleholders and embroidered Pierre Frey fabrics, interspersed with rare rattan designs from the Atelier Vime catalog by Charlotte Perriand, Gio Ponti and Robert Mallet-Stevens. With the recent launch of Maison Vime, a seasonal boutique and showroom located on the other side of their garden, within sight of the Rhône River, Rauzy and Watson have appointed some of their own furniture and artwork to give the new space a similar look and feel as their home. It's the company's first and only physical outpost, and a way of sharing the founders' *art de vivre* with visitors without having to give up their privacy.

Rauzy and Watson now consider Vallabrègues their main residence, though they keep properties in Paris and rural Brittany. "This is our house of the *farniente* and the sweetness of life; a place where we eat, nap and read by the pool," says Rauzy. "Since it was intended to be our holiday house, it was never really designed for working, but we find it easy to get creative here."

The couple likes to work from a stone-topped table in their large, wood-beamed kitchen. Though the vocation appears to have found Rauzy and Watson upon moving to the countryside, Atelier Vime still resonates with their careers in sustainability and styling in the city. The latter is visible in the brand's meticulous art direction, while Rauzy's expertise in water systems has encouraged them to start cultivating their own wicker at their Breton farm, using a traditional method that requires no extra water,

other than the dew that collects on the plant.

"We work together in a very democratic way," explains Rauzy. "There are no rules, really. We're both involved in every aspect of the business." Their collaborations with renowned designers, such as Pierre Yovanovitch and David Netto, have inspired the

(above)
Books stacked next to an old fireplace. The couple use the home year-round, alternating between their properties in Paris, Provence and Brittany.

couple to start their own interior design side gig, where they create rustic-elegant spaces for a small clientele.

The house—and by extension the brand—is also a showcase for a life's collection of antiques. Rauzy grew up amid the *antiquaires* of Paris' rue des Saints-Pères, where the couple have an apartment, and he developed a penchant for colorful Suzani textiles while working in Russia and Uzbekistan. "A lot of the objects we have were handed down from our families," says

Watson, who is a dual British-French citizen and spent his childhood between Cameroon, the UK and his mother's native Provence.

Out of the two, it's Rauzy who finds it easier to let go of pieces. "Maybe it's because I'm older, but I'm more detached than Anthony; I like the idea of things evolving and time passing," he says. "There are of course items I wouldn't sell, but that's more because they are linked to a person or a personal story." What then would they save if their house was engulfed in flames? "Our dog, Alma," they both say without hesitation.

The real pride for them, however, lies beyond their collection and their dog. Rauzy and Watson get a lot of satisfaction from seeing the craft revival that they have triggered in the region. The profession of the wicker worker was virtually extinct by the 1960s, leaving only a handful of specialists. Now, a number of ateliers in and around the village—as well as across France— are reopening their doors to manufacture place mats, lampshades and other wicker items for Atelier Vime.

"Vallabrègues has been getting more attention in the past few years than in the 50 before that; we now have people from all over the world coming to our village to learn about this almost-forgotten *savoir-faire*," says Rauzy. "It's bringing a lot of satisfaction to the local community of artisans to be selling their items elsewhere than at the regional markets."

Rauzy and Watson know most of the craftsmen personally and regularly visit them at their ateliers to supervise production. "We want to make sure we respect the heritage of rural Provence and steer away from the folkloric," Rauzy adds. He's referring to Atelier Vime, but he could just as well be talking about the home he and Watson have lovingly created for themselves.

(overleaf)   The couple recruited Elise Orrier, a specialist in natural paints, to create lime paint for the rooms using local pigments.

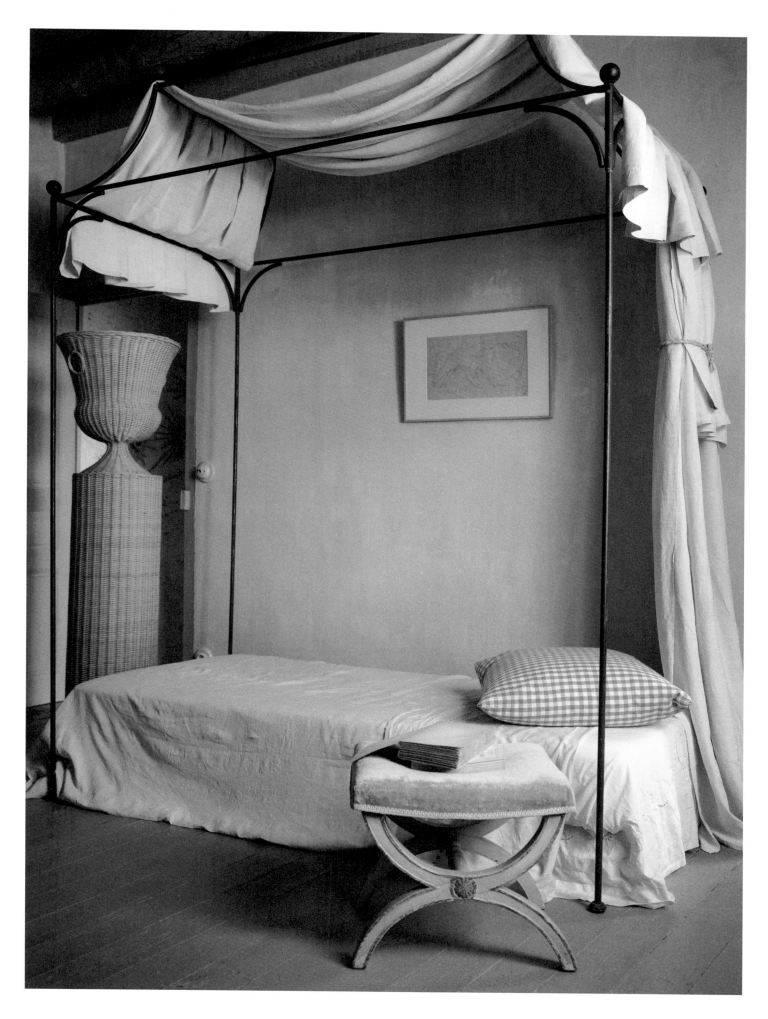

" I like the idea of things evolving and time passing."

(opposite)   Alma, the couple's Andalusian Podenco, lounges on a swan neck daybed in the summer salon. An 18th-century Aubusson tapestry hangs above.

Can community ever
be manufactured?

ESSAY:
KEEPING UP
APPEARANCES

Words
ALLYSSIA ALLEYNE

Community is just a direct debit away. At a time when we are increasingly detached from one another (a 2015 study found only 13% of Brits aged 25 to 39 knew the names of their five closest neighbors), a glut of premium spaces have emerged that count connection and collaboration among their amenities—from coworking spaces and co-living complexes to members' clubs and lifestyle hotels. Buy in and you're not just gaining access to a space: You're getting the chance to be a part of something bigger.

In these spaces, it's assumed, you'll find people with similar interests, values and backgrounds. You'll work, drink or go to gong baths together. However, a skepticism seems to follow. On a company homepage or investor deck, "community"—like "identity" or "family" can seem like another pillar of private life, appropriated and commodified.

The idea of selling community is nothing new. The developers of master-planned residential communities—from the UK's 20th-century garden city movement to modern suburban developments—have long lured prospective residents with the promise of community.

"It is an ideal type of community that resonates in the collective imagination, recalling a romanticized view of a small town or village setting," academics at the University of Queensland wrote in a 2008 study into contemporary planned estates in Australian suburbs. "While residents have little requirement or desire, and few excess resources, to devote to the establishment of durable social relationships or civic norms within the boundaries of the development; the process by which the developer creates an illusion, or 'sense' of community plays an important role in

" We use 'community' in so many ways, it's a really slippery term."

The question arises: Can you ever really manufacture community? Consider, for example, an internal WeWork study titled *Are Our Members Friends?*, published in 2017, which found that "the average WeWork member isn't socially connected with others in their building." Sixty-nine percent of members reported they had no friends at WeWork beyond their colleagues, and few could identify many other members by name.[1]

Our notions of community extend beyond friendship, however. "We use 'community' in so many ways, it's a really slippery term," says Clay Spinuzzi, a professor of rhetoric and writing at the University of Texas at Austin. As an example, he points to the different connotations of the word at a place of worship, a gated community, and in the LGBTQ+ community. With a concept so open to interpretation, corporate entities are given ample room to redefine it for their benefit.

the establishment of a subjective sense of ontological security for residents."

"This outcome," they continue, "is to the benefit of both resident and developer. The developer's brand and reputation is enhanced and the resident remains unencumbered by any need for commitment to a local 'commons.'"

(1)   According to the book *The Cult of We: WeWork, Adam Neumann, and the Great Startup Delusion*, when WeWork staff heard the call "Activate the space" during visits by investors, they would make the coworking space look as if it was full by pretending to be members.

In Spinuzzi's experience, would-be community-creators often struggle to concretely explain what the word means to them. For a 2018 article published in the *Journal of Business and Technical Communication*, Spinuzzi and a team of researchers interviewed and observed coworkers, community managers and other employees at coworking spaces in the United States, Italy and Serbia to find out what "community" meant to them in practical terms.

Across the board, participants used the term inconsistently, encompassing everything from socializing and knowledge-sharing to merely working alongside another person; and members seemed divided in what they wanted out of their community experience. Where one person wanted companionship, Spinuzzi says, another just wanted a quiet place to work without their dogs interrupting.

" I'm not sure that community is a thing you can sell—it's more of a feeling."

What the operators of these spaces offer, he suggests, is the opportunity for individuals to have their diverse needs met in an environment that feels both personal and collaborative, and within structures they neither have to develop nor sustain—conditions that don't often emerge organically. "There's a lot of what is sometimes called mutual adjustment.... I think a community manager, or a community team, has to be involved in that to make sure that everybody's still pointed in the same direction," Spinuzzi says.

Ben Prevezer is the cofounder and CEO of boutique co-living company Mason & Fifth, which currently operates a 28-unit space in southeast London (most rooms are leased for at least three months, but others can be booked by the night). He says he is acutely aware of the distrust of commoditized communities.

"I'm not sure that community is a thing you can sell—it's more of a feeling," he says. "We're not like, 'Here is a community for you to plug straight into and become part of.'" Initially, Prevezer saw the company's role as curating experiences, such as supper clubs, craft nights and talks, but he now considers it to be more a case of facilitating the community to do this themselves. While plans do still come from the top (he's taking the lead on an upcoming wild swimming and camping trip), Mason & Fifth regularly hosts events instigated and led by residents, including a photography class and life drawing.

Patch, a group of coworking spaces with three locations in southeast England, is on a similar mission to create hubs for community-building, though its definition of community extends beyond its fee-paying members. "One way that we frame what we're trying to do is that we want to become a lighthouse for local life—to be a space in the community where people can come to connect, to discover new ideas, to work, to socialize," says Paloma Strelitz, Patch's head of product and creative director.

A cofounder of the Turner Prize–winning collective Assemble, best known for its socially minded public projects, Strelitz believes Patch's spaces should support local initiatives to foster community, rather than create separate siloed communities with its members.[2] To that end, the team has adopted an open-door policy, inviting the public and local organizations to use their facilities for free or at reduced rates, subsidized by the fee-paying tenants.

"The first and fundamental point of learning from my Assemble experience is that there are fantastic people everywhere you go doing interesting and engaging things," Strelitz says. "Every place [Patch goes] to, we understand that it is our responsibility to reach out and build relationships."

Still, for all of their positive intentions, such spaces, driven by profit and primed to scale, can feel contrived. Perhaps, on a fundamental level, we think of communities as more, well, communal, in the way of a kibbutz or a co-op, or a particularly cohesive house share. Rather than a top-down approach—where members pay for and rely on outside agents to facilitate connection for their own gain—should community members be working together to determine their needs and find ways to address them collaboratively?

This is the model embraced by the artist-led Cubitt gallery in Islington, north London, which counts Peter Doig, Chris Ofili and Ingrid Pollard as alums. The 32 members renting its affordable studio spaces each take on a job, such as building maintenance or fundraising, to help keep costs down, and further the organization's mission through participation in internal committees. Similarly, residents of the Old Hall Community, housed in a former friary in Suffolk, pool resources, dine together, and put in 15 hours of work a week to maintain the house and its gardens.

This model can have surprising longevity. Cubitt and the Old Hall have been going strong since 1991 and 1974 respectively, while the Oberlin Student Cooperative Association—one of the largest co-ops in North America—has provided at-cost room and board to the Ohio college's student body for nearly 75 years.[3]

Whether corporate-run communities can ever deliver something similar is, Spinuzzi explains, difficult to determine. "Authenticity, kind of like community, is really hard to pin down. I think people are going to have their own definitions, and those definitions evolve over time," he says. "It depends on what the [community managers and members] mean by community, and if those ideas are synchronized."

As is always the case in the free market, the value of such communities has less to do with the product itself, than with what consumers take away from it. But a degree of mutual investment could be essential for delivering long-lasting personal returns.

(2)   One example of Assemble's work is the Granby Winter Garden, which saw the transformation of two derelict row houses in a declining area of Liverpool. The indoor garden they created in the shell of the two buildings is freely accessible to local residents and the wider neighborhood.

(3)   OSCA is entirely separate from Oberlin College, but all OSCA member-owners are Oberlin College students. Members are responsible for almost every task, including cooking, cleaning, purchasing food, scheduling work charts, enforcing food safety, sitting on the board of directors and more.

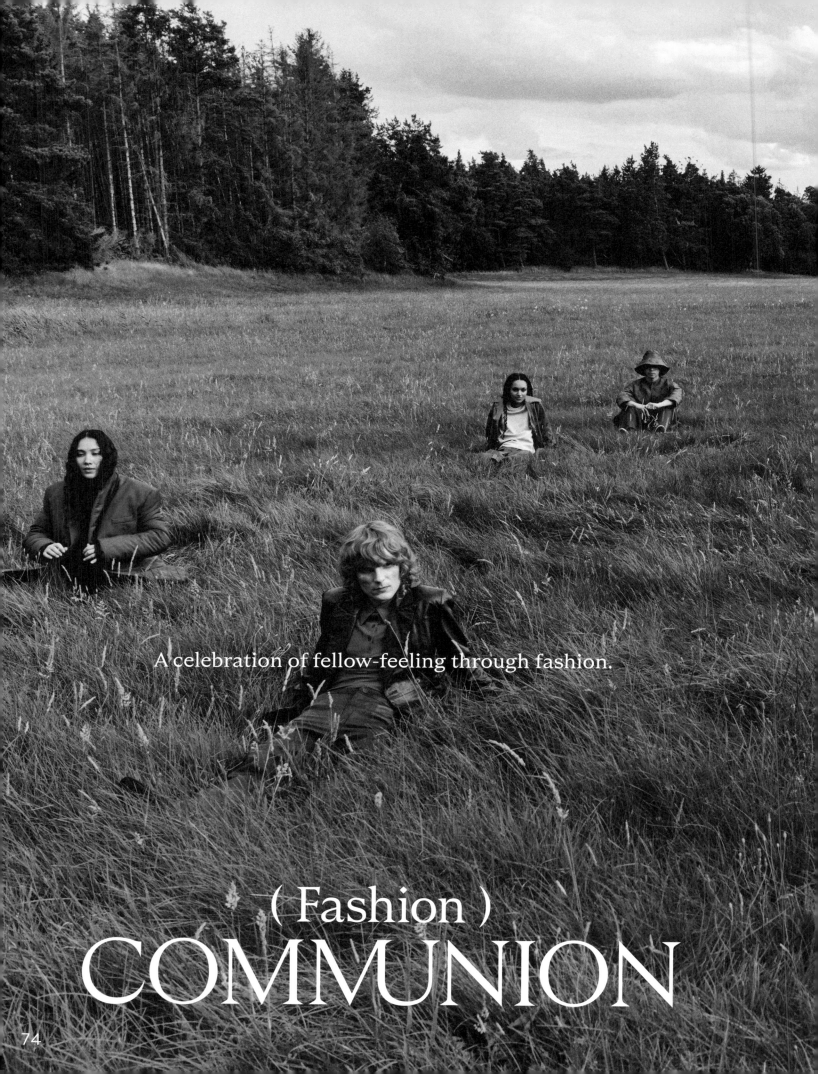

A celebration of fellow-feeling through fashion.

(Fashion)
COMMUNION

Photos EDGAR BERG Styling JULIA QUANTE

(previous) Clockwise: Celine wears a top and skirt by HERMÈS and a jacket by FILIPPA K. Idrica wears a suit by BALLY. Alero wears a trench coat by WILLIAM FAN. John wears a T-shirt by OUR LEGACY and trousers by KENZO. Hanna wears a shirt by MAWO and vintage trousers. Azza wears a suit by COMME DES COSTUMES and a shirt by ODEEH. Hannes wears a suit by GESTUZ and a polo shirt by FILIPPA K. Momo wears an outfit by CHRISTIAN WIJNANTS. Miriam wears a coat and trousers by ODEEH and a T-shirt by FUNDUS. Tru wears a coat, hat and trousers by ODEEH and a vest by BY MALENE BIRGER.

Art Direction: Christian Møller Andersen. DOP: Sheldon Harris. Production: Franziskus Dornhege.

(opposite)   Idrica wears a suit by BALLY. Tru wears a vest by BY MALENE BIRGER.
(below)
Left to Right: John wears a jacket by TOMMY HILFIGER. Hannes wears a top and pants by NEHERA. Alero wears a sweater by ICEBERG and vintage trousers. Idrica wears a top by ARKET and trousers by & OTHER STORIES. Miriam wears a dress by VALENTINO. Celine wears a dress by COMME DES COSTUMES.

(above) John wears a T-shirt by OUR LEGACY and trousers by KENZO. All other models are styled as per page 76.

(opposite)   Clockwise: Celine wears a dress by COMME DES COSTUMES. Azza wears a vest and trousers by CLOSED. Hannes wears a top and pants by NEHERA.
Hanna wears a skirt and sweater by CHRISTIAN WIJNANTS. Idrica wears a top by ARKET and trousers by & OTHER STORIES. John wears a jacket by
TOMMY HILFIGER, a T-shirt by TIGER OF SWEDEN and trousers by 7 FOR ALL MANKIND. Momo wears a dress by BY MALENE BIRGER. Alero
wears a sweater by ICEBERG and vintage trousers.

Hair: Noriko Takayama. Makeup: Paloma Brytscha using Schwanen Garten and Glossier.

Front to Back: Hanna wears a hoodie by DRIES VAN NOTEN. Celine wears an outfit by MAX MARA. Azza wears a suit by BOSS. Momo wears a sweater by ARKET. Miriam wears a dress by WILLIAM FAN. Alero wears a dress by IVY OAK.

(above)   Tru wears an top by MAGLIANO.
(opposite) Clockwise: Tru wears an outfit by MAGLIANO. Alero wears an outfit by WILLIAM FAN. John wears a T-shirt by MAWO and a jacket and trousers by PAUL
SMITH. Miriam wears an outfit by PRADA. Momo wears a knit by OUR LEGA   and a T-shirt and leggings by FILIPPA K.

Words
EMILY MAY

Angela
TRIMBUR:

Styling
HEATHER REST

AN
AL-OUT
TOUR DE
FORCE.

(above)   Trimbur wears a top and skirt by SIMONE ROCHA and shoes by LABUCQ.
(previous)   She wears a bodysuit and tights by WOLFORD.
(right)   She wears a top by MELITTA BAUMEISTER.
(far right) She wears a jacket by ACNE STUDIOS and shorts by ISSEY MIYAKE.

Angela Trimbur's first experience of community was at her mother's dance studio in Bensalem, Pennsylvania.[1] "I spent so much time there, it was basically my second home," says the actor, choreographer, writer and dancer, who's speaking to me on a video call from LA, having narrowly escaped a hurricane on a weekend road trip. Outside of classes, Trimbur's mom would get people together for themed parties or to paint props and sets for recitals. "I felt like I was always hosting people. I became a little community leader by proxy."

This community would disappear suddenly, however, just before Trimbur was supposed to start middle school. After speaking with the parent of a student who was a Jehovah's Witness, her mother became "swirly-eyed" for the religion. She closed the studio and convinced Trimbur and her younger sister to be homeschooled.

Though initially excited about the prospect, the sisters slowly realized that they weren't allowed to hang out with anybody other than people at the church.[2] As time went by, they became desperate to go back to school, running to the window every afternoon at 3:15 to see their old school bus go by and begging their mom to let them return to class. At home most of the day, the Trimbur sisters' world narrowed to their house and backyard.

Trimbur now has mixed feelings about this period of her childhood. While she describes feeling trapped—10 years ago, she used this word as the title of a one-woman show reflecting on her time as a homeschooled Jehovah's Witness—she recognizes that everything she went through during that time has informed the arc of her career and made her into the person she is today. "I like who I am right now," she says assuredly.

(1)   The inclusive ethos of Trimbur's mother's dance studio, Pitter Patter Dance Studio, had a formative impact on Trimbur and can be seen in many of the classes she runs today.
(2)   The Trimbur sisters named their homeschool "Cornerstone Academy" and for the first month wore uniforms before deciding that pajamas were better.

Hair & Makeup: Nicole Maguire. Set Design: Lee Levy.

For one, the isolation cultivated Trimbur's love of acting. "I was performing all the time, pretending to be at parties, making out with my reflection..." she recalls. Starved of creative input, Trimbur and her sister found inspiration in unlikely places, from flowers growing in the garden to the rhythm of door knockers during their door-to-door preaching visits. They played clock radios secretly under their bedsheets, and were once even snuck Tori Amos, Hole and Fiona Apple albums through the window by an old school friend.

Eventually, the family was disfellowshipped from the religion due to a tryst Trimbur had with a boy at the church.[3] "My mom was really frustrated with the punishment. She was like, 'This is a cult, let's get out.'" Trimbur was able to attend her senior year, which she describes as the most fun she'd had in her life. "I had zero social anxiety. I was the class clown."

After a short stint at the Fashion Institute of Technology in New York, Trimbur moved to LA and began taking acting classes. Once on the West Coast, her childhood experiences set her on a quest to find, join and create as many communities as possible to make up for lost time. "I always longed for any sort of friendship," she says, attributing her yearning to having not been able to forge relationships during school. One of the first groups Trimbur joined in LA was a women's recreational basketball team, the Pistol Shrimps, which she discovered on Facebook. Named after the innocuous-looking sea creatures that release a flurry of bubbles to stun prey into submission, the team included famous faces such as *The White Lotus*

" Seeing that I can create spaces where I can help people in a playful way is amazing."

actor Aubrey Plaza, and would later become the subject of a 2016 documentary directed by Brent Hodge. "I was the silly one," laughs Trimbur, describing how she'd do cartwheels in the middle of the court during gameplay. "I had no basketball skills."

Trimbur's irreverent—a word she uses repeatedly—approach to basketball also extended to the routines she choreographed and performed with the L.A. City Municipal Dance Squad, an all-female group she established after watching a halftime performance at a Lakers game. "I wanted to do my own version of it," she says. The weekly routines she choreographed featured silly humor, throwback songs and partner work that parodied professional sports dance teams. "What I love about halftime dancing is that you have two minutes to infect the audience with joy, get them laughing and keep the energy up."

90

Trimbur's love of imbuing others with energy was also the motivator behind her event series A Slightly Guided Dance Party. Inspired by seeing the relief on guests' faces when "Throw Your Hands in The Air" by Outkast came on at house parties—a song effectively telling them how to move—she wondered, *How would it be if everyone had permission to be silly in a specific way, song by song?* As a result, an instructional, task-based format became the basis for her now-famous dance sessions, hosted at venues ranging from LA's Museum of Contemporary Art to a private wedding reception. "I also did a Valentine's Day–themed one for couples in New York," she says. "It was very dance therapy–based. Seeing that I can create spaces where I can help people in a playful way is amazing."

Being part of all these different groups has helped Trimbur define what makes a good community: "It's about holding space and having empathy for each other's personal growth," she says. "It's also confidence contagion. Whatever activity you're doing, you're encouraging each other to shine." Her dance squad made her fall in love with the idea of sisterhood. "It was almost like my own little sorority," she says. "There are so many hoops women have to jump through just for any sort of respect. When we come together, it feels like we have each other's backs. That became really necessary for me."

In 2018, Trimbur was diagnosed with breast cancer and her sisterhood became more necessary than ever before. "The first thought that went through my head was, *How am I going to do this?*

(above)   Trimbur wears a top by BODE.
(opposite) She wears a top by MARYAM NASSIR ZADEH, a dress by YUZEFI and shoes by STELLA MCCARTNEY.
(previous) She wears a dress by REJINA PYO.

I can't work. What am I going to do?" Immediately, the Pistol Shrimps set up a GoFundMe to support her financially, and friends started a schedule to make sure she always had someone to take her to medical appointments. One would turn up in costume and sing songs in the hospital waiting rooms, creating, as she puts it, "a kind of Patch Adams energy."

Though she was initially reluctant to do so, Trimbur documented her cancer journey openly on social media. "When you're an actor, you're so hungry for opportunity. I was scared to announce that I had a sickness that might take me away from jobs," she explains. But after becoming drained by having to repeat the sentence "I have breast cancer" what felt like thousands of times, she decided Instagram was the easiest way to save herself from more of the same "dreaded" exchanges. "At first, it was like a bulletin board of updates for my friends," she explains. "But then people started sharing my account with other people that they knew were going through breast cancer. It was a win-win."

In Trimbur's hands, social media became a force for good. Saddened by seeing women having to attend appointments alone during the pandemic, she set up a digital support group on the video messaging app Marco Polo. The success of the platform, which is now used by around 500 women, also led to Trimbur hosting *Good Support*, an online series in which she talks candidly with other survivors about their experiences. "I almost became some sort of torch carrier for young women going through breast cancer," she says. "I didn't mind; it made me feel like there was a purpose to all the pain."

After a long period of not being able to dance to her max due to surgeries—she describes making hand shadows and foot dances in bed during periods of healing—Trimbur dove back into dance in

(3)   Jehovah's Witnesses are disfellowshipped if a judicial committee decides they are unrepentant after committing a serious sin. According to *The Watchtower*, the official publication of the Jehovah's Witnesses, 1 in every 100 members are disfellowshipped each year. Adherents are forbidden to have contact with anyone who has been excluded from the faith.

a big way, relocating to New York in 2021 with only $3,000 in the bank and not knowing anyone. "Thank God I did, I'm in love with New York!" she says, enthusing about her *Flashdance*-style loft in Bushwick, and the fact that, unlike in LA, she can go to a dance performance every night.

Trimbur is still getting surgeries and learning about her new body as a young woman in forced menopause. "You live with it; it's a constant battle it seems," she says. But, after only two years in New York, she's already found a sense of belonging in the city's "massive" dance community, taking classes and opportunities everywhere she can. She's performed a Broadway number at a fundraiser talent show for artist-run dance space Pageant, won Montez Press Radio's fifth annual karaoke contest, made friends with a community of line dancers in the back of an East Village Ukrainian restaurant and choreographed *Slanted! Enchanted!*, a musical based on indie rock band Pavement's debut album. Her secret to making lots of friends fast? Never be afraid of rejection, and always follow up on vague invitations.

> " Nostalgia is a way into your body through memories that you need to unlock, hold onto or expand on."

True to form, Trimbur has started establishing new communities, in the form of her own dance classes at venues including the New York City Center and the Martha Graham Center of Contemporary Dance.[4] Her first, and most well-known, is Thirteen, which forgoes the intimidating and mathematical approach of "5, 6, 7, 8" dance counts in favor of encouraging participants to connect with their inner child by screaming, running around to Britney Spears' "Sometimes" or pretending to come out of the womb to Lady Gaga's "Born This Way."

Thirteen, like all of Trimbur's classes, is rooted in make-believe and nostalgia. "At the beginning of class, I always say that we're all best friends, we're in a backyard and we're going to show our parents this silly routine we're doing before dinner," she says. "Nostalgia is a way into your body through memories that you need to unlock, hold onto or expand on." It also informs the way Trimbur and her students dress for class—in leotards and slouch socks. "It makes you more excited to attend when you have these outfits to wear. Looking at yourself in the mirror is like seeing an old version of yourself, or a version of yourself you wish you could be."

(4)   Founded in 1926, the Martha Graham Center of Contemporary Dance is the oldest continually performing contemporary dance company in the world. It teaches the "Graham technique" of contemporary dance which was developed by its founder and is considered the cornerstone of American modern dance.

Off the back of Thirteen, Trimbur has created various other teaching concepts, including "TRIM/BUR(N)," an '80s VHS workout-inspired fitness session, and "balletcore," which invites dancers to enjoy the aesthetics and music of ballet while leaving the intimidating perfection behind. She wants to make ballet "a playful place," particularly for anyone who quit when they were younger because they had the wrong ankles, grew boobs or just felt like they didn't fit into the competitive scene. Assuming the persona of a director, she calls her students her "company," leading them through a reimagined ballet barre featuring sloppy fifth positions, and instructing them to lick the air and perform chest pops before teaching them an "irreverent" routine to *Swan Lake* or Beethoven. "There are ballet moves in there, but we're doing it differently," she says. "In the same way that people aren't in the NBA but still wear jerseys and play basketball, I wanted to create a world where people can pretend they're professional ballerinas."

Though she's already instigated many community-building projects in her new city, Trimbur still has plenty of ambitions for the future: She chats excitedly about her plans for dance camps and Christmas recitals, as well as her goal to choreograph for Broadway. "I'm also talking to the Metropolitan Transportation Authority about doing something with them. I want to do a rat king ballet in the subway," she says.

> " I'm talking to the Metropolitan Transportation Authority.... I want to do a rat king ballet in the subway."

More than anything, Trimbur has resolved to remain open to whatever life throws at her. "You just have to be curious—that's your way into other people's hearts, as well as your own," she says, paraphrasing her acting teacher. She recalls another quote from Twyla Tharp, a seminal figure in modern dance whose melding together of contemporary, jazz, ballet and even aerobics has been a great influence.[5]

"She says that you've got to bend with the wind, to keep it moving," Timbur explains, adding that this philosophy—which she references in her Instagram bio—has informed her approach to life in recent years. "You get cancer? You get hit by a global pandemic? You lose an opportunity? You bend with the wind. It's the best way to live in a way that doesn't feel limiting," she says. "You go where the wind takes you. You dance with the wind."

[5]   One of Tharp's most famous works is "Nine Sinatra Songs" from 1982—a series of nine meditations on relationships choreographed to Frank Sinatra's music. At the age of 81, Tharp briefly revived the show in October 2022 at the New York City Center.

(above)   Trimbur wears a bodysuit by SIMONE ROCHA.

Words
DAPHNÉE DENIS
Photos
IRIS HUMM

"I make things, I'm doing things—that's all there is to it." The Barcelona-based art director and interior designer Gabriel Escámez is explaining his work as the head of Cobalto Studio, the multidisciplinary creative agency that he founded in 2015. Escámez is certainly a creative force, turning his hand to photography, art direction, various forms of design and editing, but there might be a little more to his endeavors than he makes out.

In addition to Cobalto Studio, which provides interior design, art direction and set design for high-end clients, there is La Cobalta—which Escámez describes as "the soul of Cobalto"—a brand that produces objects, ceramics, lighting and books inspired by the culture of the Mediterranean. There is also the Cobalto Archive, a collection of over 2,000 pieces of modern and contemporary furniture that are available to rent.

And Escámez is in the process of creating another website for all the projects that don't fit into Cobalto or La Cobalta.

Tying it all together, he says, is a common thread of authenticity and tradition: "I can't do anything if there's no substance—if I can't look at the cultural baggage of a given thing and project something contemporary onto it."

It's an approach that has defined Cobalto Studio's ad campaigns for Nina Ricci and set design for Loewe; the styling for photo shoots in various editions of *Vogue* and the boutique stores designed for French brand Sessùn. Meanwhile, with the products he curates for La Cobalta, Escámez pursues an ongoing "cultural investigation" into rapidly disappearing rites and craftsmanship of the Mediterranean, such as with a series of earthenware plates painted by Spanish artist Marria Pratts.

A sea of tranquil designs inspired by the Mediterranean coastline.

(At Work With)

GABRIEL ESCÁMEZ

FEATURES

" I don't want to take on projects that don't nurture me."

FEATURES

La Cobalta is also where some of Escámez's passion projects see the light of day, such as *Balearics*, a series of books published in 2021 that explore the art, food and folklore of the Balearic Islands (Majorca, Minorca, Ibiza and Formentera). The project was five years in the making and he sold the books at a loss, but Escámez fondly remembers an exhausting shooting schedule and "the magic of all these insane stories."

"What resonates with me is seeing what makes us unique, but then also what we share around the Mediterranean basin," he says. It's an interest that is central to his work—the name "Cobalto" derives from the cobalt-blue pigment that has been used traditionally to paint doors and shutters across the Mediterranean.

As a child, Escámez created and photographed still lifes, and his father, an industrial engineer, taught him to build mechanisms and maquettes to play with. Later, he studied fine art before switching to interior design at the Deià School of Art and Design in Barcelona. But the experience with fine art contributed to his holistic vision of creativity. "Sketching, designing a chair or imagining a three-story space, it's all the same to me," he says. "I never saw the difference, and everything feels the same because my approach remains the same."

Escámez's work draws heavily from Catalan rationalist architecture, which put simplicity and functionality at the heart of design. He regrets that the popularity of the new Mediterranean style of interiors has deprived them of their meaning. "I see some people that just take the aesthetic and there's no functionality, they just use the same three materials over and over again without understanding what it's about. It reminds me of what happens with Nordic style, which has also been so poorly interpreted," he says.

Even if he is known for using a sober, neutral palette—earthy tones and natural materials set against white backgrounds—Escámez considers humor and irony essential to his work. This is apparent in the design of Madrid's trendiest cheese shop, Formaje, where giant wheels of cheese are elevated to the status of sculptures in a pared-back interior of granite and dark wood. The kitsch of the Barcelona Olympics in 1992 is also an important reference for Escámez, who remembers watching the event as a child; his friends still give him toy figurines of Cobi, the Cubist-style mascot (he appreciates the idea but tells me with a laugh that he has enough).

When we speak, Escámez is spending the summer at his country house in southern Catalonia—a welcome respite from city life. The last year was hectic, he tells me, and put many things into perspective. Cobalto Studio moved into a 10,700-square-foot space in 2022, where they can now fit their archive and equipment. "I used to live right next to work, but now I'm really thankful that I have to walk 20 minutes to get there," he says. "It gives me space to rest, to observe the city every morning. Occasionally I even sit on a swing I walk by every day."

In his personal life, grieving several family members who recently passed away at a young age was a wake-up call, he tells me, and led him to distance himself from certain jobs. "There are some projects in set design and art direction that I'm going to try not to take on anymore. Some clients come to you with one specific result in mind, and that's all they want," he says. "I don't want to take on projects that don't nurture me. I just want to do whatever feels right to me, what makes me feel at peace."

La Cobalta is currently working on a clothing line inspired by traditional Mediterranean garments. The idea, Escámez explains, is to create "neo-rites"—invented traditions that become real over time. He speaks about Cara, Cobalto's take on the traditional *cabezudo*, an oversized ceramic head worn during folkloric processions, which simultaneously looks backward and forward: "Toward the future and back to our cultural heritage; I think that's the best way to describe our focus with Cobalto and La Cobalta."

Escámez may tell me self-deprecatingly that he's just "doing things," but he knows where he's going, and where he's come from.

(previous)
The furniture archive at the Cobalto
Studio offices in Sant Martí de Provençals
neighborhood of Barcelona.

(right)
A comfortable lounge area at Cobalto Studio,
where the team can relax.

(Interview)
ANNIE
RAUWERDA

What the depths of Wikipedia can teach us all about community.
Words TOM FABER Photos EMMA TRIM

With almost seven million articles—in English alone—covering every subject imaginable, Wikipedia can teach you about more than just academic subjects and pop culture. If you're willing to dig, it will also reveal to you the true extent of human absurdity.

Plumbing the online encyclopedia's strangest corners is the specialty of 23-year-old Annie Rauwerda, whose social media account Depths of Wikipedia became a viral sensation over the pandemic. She unearthed pages most users would never come across, like an entry on "extreme ironing," a sport practiced on mountaintops and motorways that "combines the thrills of an extreme outdoor activity with the satisfaction of a well-pressed shirt"; the "bald-hairy pattern" which dictates that Russian leaders alternate according to their hairlines; and the inspiring story of Diego the tortoise, who "had so much sex he saved his species."

Rauwerda's unerring ability to identify humor in this repository of world knowledge has gained her over a million followers. Yet beneath the jokes, her posts also draw attention to the dizzying human achievement that is Wikipedia, a noncommercial site, maintained mostly by volunteers, that stands as a monument to old-school internet idealism and the altruistic capabilities of online communities.

Growing up in Grand Rapids, Michigan, Rauwerda developed a conversational style best described as "internet-y," talking at the lightning speed of fiber-optic cable, with sardonic quips and meme-worthy asides. Her innate attunement to online sensibility has garnered large followings not just for Depths of Wikipedia and its incarnation as a live comedy show, but also for last summer's Perpetual Stew Club, a community cooking project in New York where a single stew was continually eaten and replenished for two months, attracting a growing community of friends, neighbors and even international media.

Speaking from her home in Brooklyn, where she is working on a book about Wikipedia, Rauwerda shares what she has learned about creating and maintaining community, both online and in real life.

TOM FABER: What was your introduction to Wikipedia?

ANNIE RAUWERDA: I'm 23—just a few months older than Wikipedia itself, so I don't really remember life without it. When I was a teenager I would edit pages, fixing typos or dead links. I didn't know anybody else doing it, but there was a big "edit" button, so it felt like a normal thing to do if you saw a mistake.

TF: What are the ingredients for a post you'd share on Depths of Wikipedia?

AR: I tend to think it's funny when lowbrow topics are discussed with formal encyclopedic language. One example is the first-ever "man walks into a bar" joke, from ancient Sumer. It doesn't really make sense to us now; the meaning has been lost, but the words remain, and I think that absurdity is funny.

TF: Do you have a favorite from your posts?

AR: The list of "sexually active popes" is a classic.

TF: How many sexually active popes are there?

AR: More than 20. In the first few hundred years of the papacy, popes were allowed to have sex, and celibacy was only obligatory after the Second Lateran Council in the 12th century. That explains why a lot of the early popes were sexually active, but there were still a bunch afterward who broke the rule.

TF: Clearly you retain this information; it's not just about the humor.

AR: Maybe three years ago I loved the idea of trivia, but I can only talk about sexually active popes so many times before I go crazy. Now I'm way more interested in Wikipedia itself, how it works, the culture, the editing.

TF: What do you like about it?

AR: It's just really smart, diligent people who embody the spirit of volunteerism.

TF: Do you see your humorous posts as a way to get people interested in the more serious side of Wikipedia?

AR: Yeah. A researcher from the London School of Economics did a study showing that after I post a Wikipedia page on Twitter, views and edits on that article go way up, and many people who contribute there for the first time go on to make more edits that are helpful and constructive. So I hope that I inspire people to get involved.

TF: Do you think Wikipedia has anything to teach us about managing IRL communities?

AR: Although it's open to everybody, very few readers actually edit Wikipedia, which is interesting. Since there are lots of rules and guidelines, when you're starting out it's hard to get the hang of things. You have to be really determined if you want to be successful. So although it's officially open to everyone, in reality it selects people that are extremely meticulous, diligent, hardworking and hellbent on doing the thing. I think that's interesting: the way it selects people without having a formal application process.

TF: Does the internet make it easier to foster and maintain communities?

AR: It makes some things easier and some things harder. Online you can have these hyperfocused communities, like the WikiProject Tropical Cyclones, which brings together people from all around the world who are obsessed

(above)
Rauwerda was named Media Contributor of the Year at the 2022 Wikimedian of the Year awards.

with documenting cyclones. It's hard to imagine that forming on a random street corner. But maybe before the internet, it was easier to make communities of local people in a neighborhood, because now they're all busy with online communities that are more specific to their interests.

TF: Tell me about Perpetual Stew Club.

AR: I'd seen an article about perpetual stew a few years ago and thought the concept was really fun, so I made a website for it and started being really active. Then other people asked to contribute, bringing vegetables and spices. It started in my house but soon there were lots of strangers, so I moved the event into the park. After a month it got so big that there were reporters everywhere, we were even broadcast on the news in San Francisco and Italy. It just got out of hand. We did it for 60 days until I had to pull the plug because I was going on vacation, and I was like: "I'm not going to get a stew-sitter."

TF: Is there some connection between Perpetual Stew and Depths of Wikipedia?

AR: One person wrote that Wikipedia is no different from a perpetual stew, in that it's a bunch of people bringing their little ingredients and making something that's free for everyone. Maybe it's related in that way.

TF: Do you think you brought anything you'd learned from Depths of Wikipedia to the Stew Club?

AR: You just have to go viral a little bit, so I tried to have a very strong online presence. Ultimately, I wasn't doing the stew completely for myself. I thought it was a fun thing and I wanted it to have an audience, so part of it was just about attention. I think it makes the whole thing more fun when there's people contributing and sharing in it.

TF: What do you think is important about building these communities? Why does it matter?

AR: I don't think it really does matter that much. But when a bunch of people show up in a random park for stew, it's like—Oh, cool, these people all wanted to leave the house and meet strangers, they just needed the impetus. I guess that's what I learned, that people do really want to show up at stuff.

TF: It's about creating the conditions to help people connect.

AR: Yeah, for sure. With both Perpetual Stew Club and Depths of Wikipedia live events, I see that people want to be a part of something. They want to be in on the joke.

(right) Rauwerda in Bushwick, Brooklyn, near the park where she organized the Perpetual Stew Club. In 2023, Rauwerda visited the longest running perpetual stew in Bangkok, Thailand, which has been cooking for nearly 50 years.

" I can only talk
about sexually active
popes so many times
before I go crazy."

III

COMMUNITY
How we come together.

Inside a Californian TikTok "content house" of a very different stripe.

The OLD

GAYS.

lot of fun, but it wasn't always like this, and they often discuss their experiences of how things used to be, bequeathing a form of institutional memory to their many followers.

Reeves recalls living in San Francisco in the early 1980s at the height of the AIDS epidemic. "A couple of years after I moved there, you started hearing all these rumors about the 'gay cancer,'" he says. "And then slowly, one by one, my close family there started dying."[2] In 1987, he discovered he was HIV positive and moved out to the desert to spend his remaining days. "I thought I was going to be dead in two years," he says. Once he was there, however, his T cells started improving, and his viral load became undetectable. "The desert gave me life," he says.

Lyons moved to Palm Springs in 2003, where he was introduced to Reeves at a movie night that Lyons was hosting at his home. They soon realized they had met before—in San Francisco in the mid-1980s. "We became really good friends," says Lyons, "and have been that way ever since."

Lyons loves being both an old gay and an Old Gay, as well as having the elder statesman status that has come with the group's fame. He also remembers a less progressive time, when it was often much tougher for young men to come out to their parents. "You just didn't do that back then," he says. "[My parents] probably would have sent me to some fancy psychiatrist in Beverly Hills to try to stop it." And then there were all the cops and city leaders who tried to drive gay men like Lyons out of Laguna Beach or bust them as they cruised LA's Griffith Park. "A lot of people have said that hearing what we were up against when we were coming out has made it easier for them to come out to their parents," he says.

The four men have created a special form of community out here in the desert, the roots of which go back decades and extend far beyond the home that Reeves and Peterson share. "If you want to call it a community, it would also include basically everybody who lives on this street," says Peterson, a former bodybuilder who moved to the desert in 2012. Here, he says, people celebrate holidays together and look out for each other.

Then there's the larger community of online fans who await the group's latest video. The Old Gays currently have nearly 11 million followers on TikTok. When asked what sorts of questions he gets from his fans, Peterson rattles off the top three: *How often do you work out? How big is it? Can I see?* "There are a lot of people who want to meet me," he says, smiling.

Even now, the level of interest can sometimes take him by surprise. "There seems to be a great curiosity in our age group from the younger generations—Gen Z, Gen X, the millennials," he says. "Whereas, the last thing I wanted to do when I was in my 20s was to be with a 60-year-old man."

Apart from the love the four have for each other, and the groovy dance routines, a big part of the group's appeal is the stories the Old Gays have gathered over the decades. These speak to a collective memory while remaining acutely personal. Like the time Martin came out to his mother after she kept asking him when he was going to get married, and how he wrote her a letter about it (he was on the road performing with a gospel group at the time), and how his brother and sister read the letter to her, and how his mom cried because she couldn't be there with him. Or the time Lyons made love to a man for the first time, in Laguna Beach, and how dirty and uncomfortable it had made him feel until he realized that all those people who had been saying that what he was doing was a sin—maybe they didn't know everything after all.

If you ask the Old Gays what they like about all of this—the meetups with celebrities, the late-found fame, all that dancing—they'll talk about how it's nice to have fun things to do at an age when fun activities of any sort tend to become scarce. But more than that, what they cherish is the family they have created, their chosen family that they care for, and which cares for them.[3]

The day before, Martin had been in the hospital, where he wasn't able to see anyone. "It was a really hard day for me," he says, "because I was totally alone." Phone calls and texts with the group sustained him. "We're family," he says. "They're here for me, and I want to be there for them." He looks over at Lyons and gives him a quick peck on the lips.

" If you want to call it a community, it would also include basically everybody who lives on this street."

(1)   The Old Gays also made an appearance on *RuPaul's Drag Race*, where they stood in for the scantily clad Pit Crew to lead a challenge.
(2)   HIV/AIDS had a devastating effect on the Old Gays' generation. In the US, by 1995, one in nine gay men had been diagnosed with AIDS.
(3)   If an LGBTQ+ person is ostracized from their biological family after coming out, a chosen family can offer support and kinship.

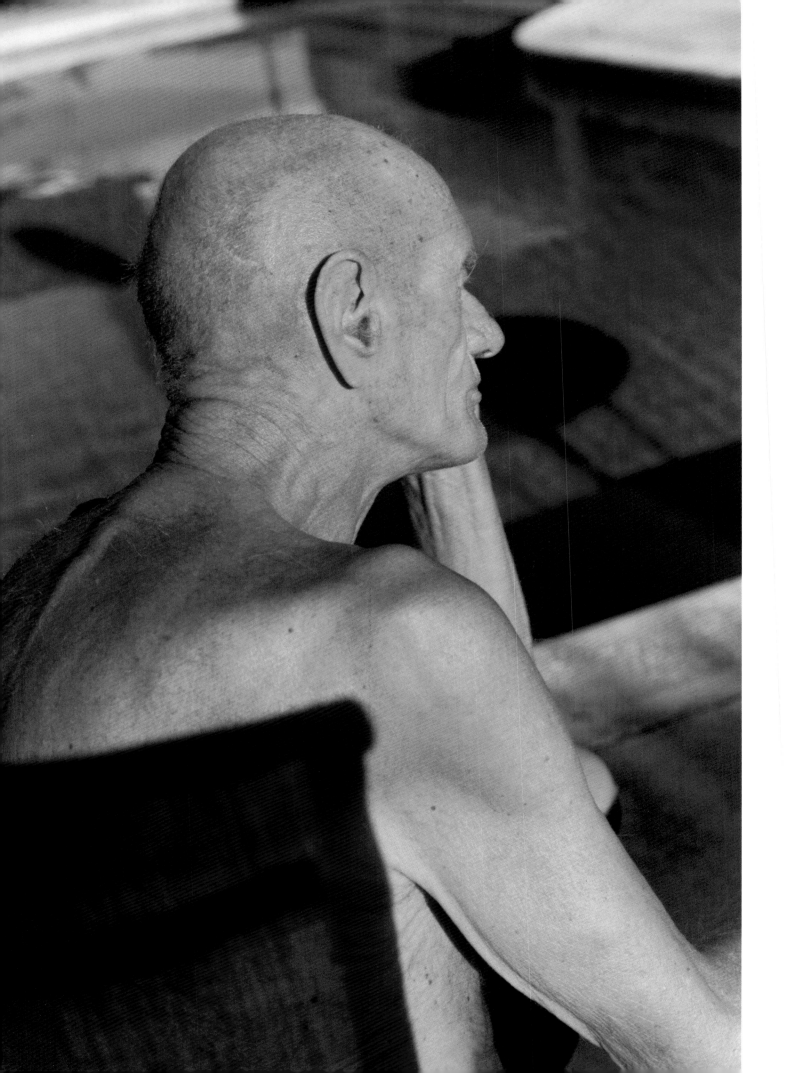

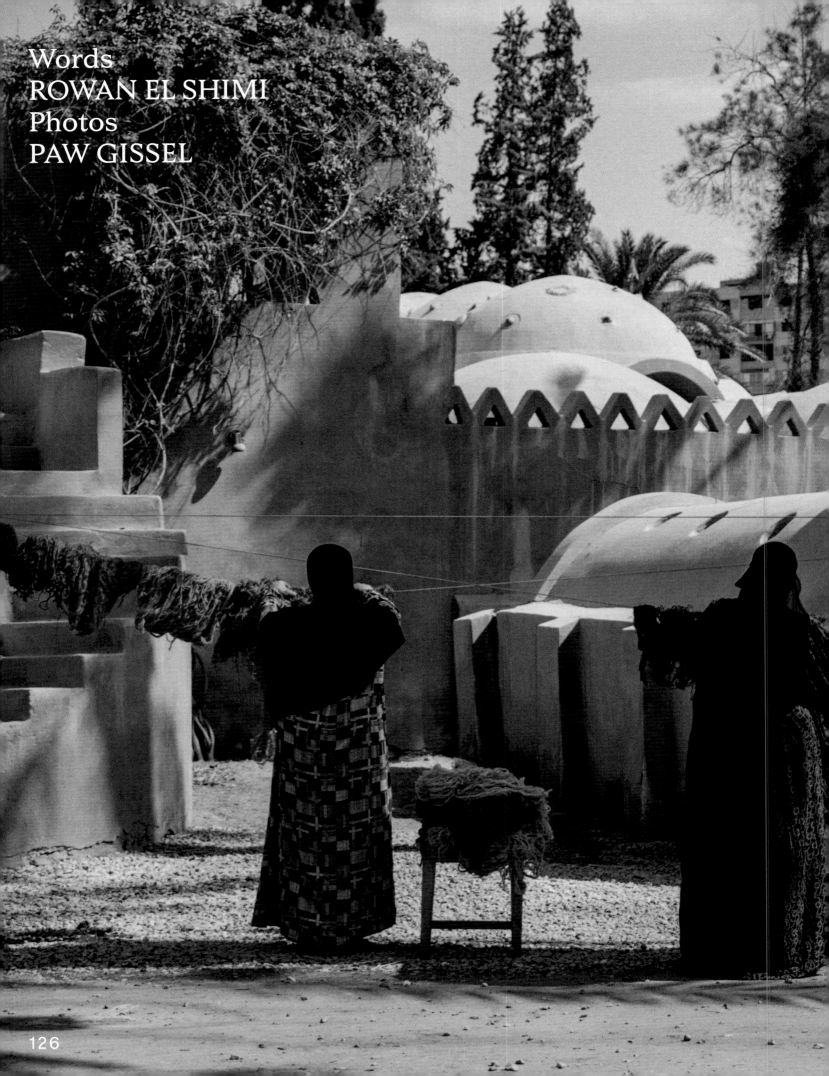

Words
ROWAN EL SHIMI
Photos
PAW GISSEL

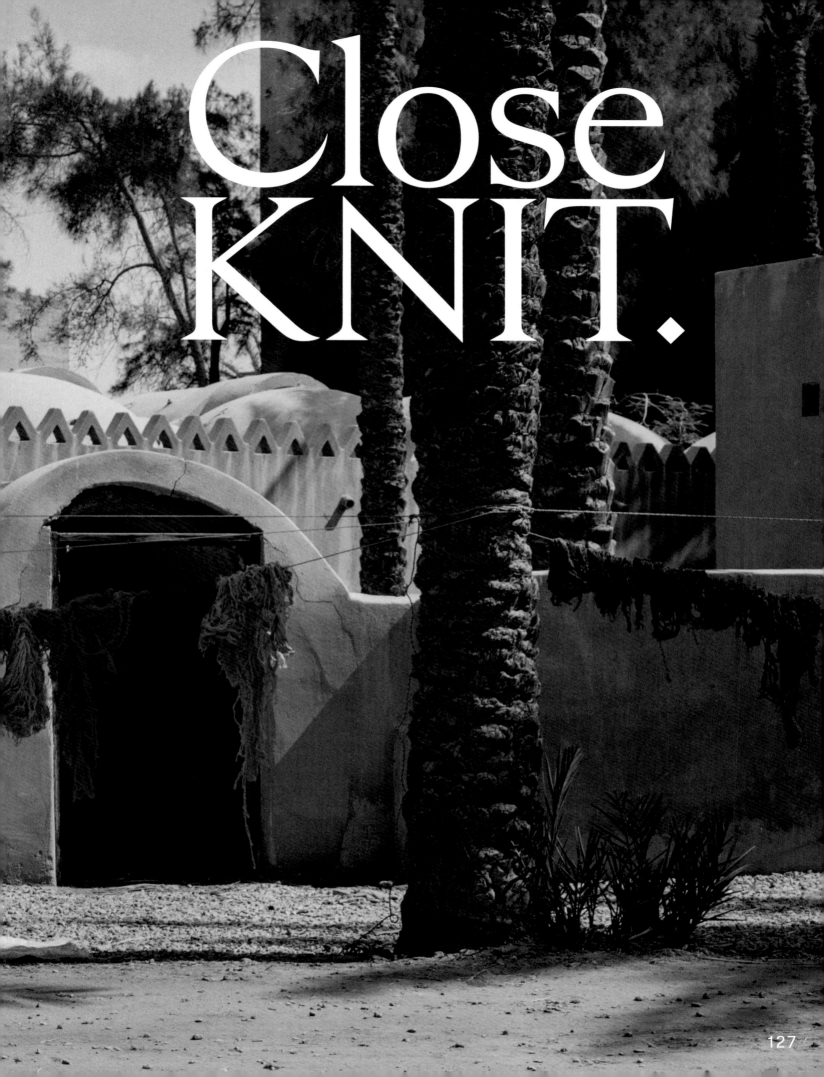

Close KNIT.

Meet the weavers keeping traditional Egyptian tapestry-making alive.

Nadia Mohamed is weaving green thread into a tapestry on the loom in front of her. Branches of palm trees layer over one another; pigeons fly off toward their brown dovecote. "The more time and dedication you give this work, the more it gives you back," the 60-year-old says as she works.

Mohamed, like the other weavers at the Ramses Wissa Wassef Art Center, began learning the craft when she was 11 years old, and it has shaped her life. "We spend more time here than we do in our own homes," she says, explaining that it is not only her source of income but the community where she feels she belongs. She started frequenting the center in 1974, joining her cousin, who was part of the first generation of weavers trained by the Egyptian architect Ramses Wissa Wassef in the 1950s.

Wissa Wassef was passionate about traditional Egyptian art and architecture and designed many celebrated public and private buildings in Cairo.[1] He established

the tapestry-making center in Harraniya—a few miles southwest of Giza—in 1951.

Born into a prominent Coptic family in Cairo in 1911, Wissa Wassef was encouraged as a child to experiment artistically, leading him to pursue not only a career in architecture but also interests in pottery, sculpture and weaving.[2] "Ramses believed that art is not a luxury but an integral part of life," says Suzanne Wissa Wassef, a potter, weaver and Ramses' eldest daughter. "Everyone has their own voice—but it can't come out unless we are free to dream."

Along with her sister, Yoanna, Suzanne currently works as part of the second generation of weavers at the center. Like Mohamed, they started at a young age—Wissa Wassef believed adults were not able to imagine freely, having been trained by school and society to think a certain way.

According to Suzanne, Wissa Wassef founded the center to prove that anyone can express themselves through art, if they are

given the opportunity. After buying a small piece of land in Harraniya, he and his wife, Sophie Habib Georgi, an art teacher, began visiting regularly, establishing a friendship with the local children. Many of them would go on to be the first generation of weavers to train at the center.

The center was built in adobe over several years and draws heavily from traditional Egyptian architecture. In 1983, it received the prestigious Aga Khan Award for Architecture for its reinvigoration of traditional mud-brick architecture and its social and cultural impact on the area.[3] Today it consists of several separate buildings with domes and a large garden dotted with flowers and trees. The surrounding farmland is used to grow plants, from which natural dyes such as reseda, dyer's rocket and madder are extracted. The property also includes several houses where the Wissa Wassef family lives. Wissa Wassef partly chose Harraniya because it didn't have an existing craft

tradition and he hoped the center would contribute to the village's economy. It was also within easy reach of his home in Cairo. Back then, the center and its surrounding agricultural land blended in seamlessly with the rural landscape. Now it sits amid the hustle and bustle of what has become an informal suburb of the Egyptian capital; the small adobe houses that once dotted the area have been replaced by high-rise buildings.

The weavers, who once took inspiration from the natural surroundings, now look to the center's garden. "Sousou [Suzanne] and I will take a walk and look at things in the garden. Once I have an idea, we discuss it and I start working directly on the loom," says Nagla Farouk. Her mother was part of the first generation of weavers to train with Wissa Wassef, and she has been coming to the center since she was seven years old. "I would go to school and then come here to play in the garden or sit with my mother— I wouldn't ever go home," she says, looking at a dried plant that she's placed on the loom for inspiration.

Wissa Wassef instructed the weavers to work directly on the loom. "If you sketch the design and then weave it, then you turn into a copying machine," Suzanne says. "You're no longer interacting with the material and you kill the imagination."

"When [the weavers] work on the loom, they develop their own language, and the slow pace of the craft allows for the imagination to be heightened," she adds, explaining that adults are not allowed to criticize the work of the children, so as not to stifle their ideas.

Besides the craft, which has been passed on to more than 120 weavers in the village, Wissa Wassef and Georgi were involved in the community in other ways. The architect's brother was a doctor and Wissa Wassef arranged for him to pay weekly visits to the village to tend to the illnesses caused by poverty and lack of access to clean water. Georgi worked on the social side of the center, running a canteen for the children and educating people about good nutrition.

In 1970, some of the weavers asked Wissa Wassef to build them houses on the property so they could live and work at the center with their families. He gave them the land as a gift and encouraged them to participate in building their own homes. Many of the weavers initially moved into the houses but, as the village became more urbanized, they moved back. The houses that were built continue to be rented to artists in residence, and one is used by Suzanne's daughter, Marianne.

"There were many challenges but there was always love. We learned from each other and respected each other; it wasn't charity," Suzanne says of the relationship between the center and the local community.

As to the question of whether there will be a third generation of weavers at the Ramses Wissa Wassef Art Center, this remains to be seen. Suzanne and her husband, Ikram Nosshi, an architect and director at the center, say they don't currently have the capacity or the same relationship with the younger generation in the village that Ramses did.

"The social structure of the village has completely changed," says Nosshi. "The generation working in the center [now] were born into a village with green spaces and livestock, and they were making bread and dairy products from scratch. Now it's an urban environment. This is the story for most of the Egyptian countryside."

Nosshi explains that with urbanization came other opportunities, whether driving tuk-tuks or working in factories or other jobs that young people often prefer to weaving, which requires patience and commitment. "It needs a new approach with this new social structure and new context. Suzanne and I are trying to make people aware of the ongoing experiment that's been taking place here in Harraniya for 71 years," he says. "It's still viable, it can empower women, and it can really serve the society."

(1)   Other notable Wissa Wassef–designed buildings in the Egyptian capital include the French School of Cairo, the church of St. Mary in Zamalek and the museum of celebrated Egyptian sculptor Mahmoud Mokhtar.

(2)   Wissa Wassef studied at the École des Beaux-Arts in Paris; his thesis project *A Potter's House in Old Cairo* received the first prize in 1935.

(3)   The jury commended the center for "the beauty of its execution, the high value of its objectives, the social impact of its activities as well as the power of its influence as an example; for its role as a pole of art and life, as represented by its location, endurance, continuity and promise."

" Ramses believed that art is not a luxury but an integral part of life."

Free W

On the road with London's Velociposse Cycling Club.

HEELERS. ◆

Words
EMILY CHAPPELL
Photos
SULEIKA MUELLER

COMMUNITY

Northwall Road rarely sees much of the typical London congestion. The road runs for just over half a mile past the velodrome in east London's Olympic Park but, being barricaded at both ends, it's frequented solely by cyclists, runners and walkers. Tonight, it's the site of a slow race between members of Velociposse Cycling Club. Half a dozen people are inching their way up the road's gentle slopes. Their faces alternate between concentration and laughter as they twitch and swerve and wobble in their attempt to stay upright and be the last person to cross the finish line. The scent of an enormous buddleia bush drifts over them, and beyond it, the rush-hour traffic of the Lea Valley Interchange roars past.

Eventually, all riders but two have put a foot down and pedaled ahead. Only Hayley Whitehorn and Megan Barclay are left, the rest of the club cheering them on from the improvised finish line. Barclay's tactic is to ride in very slow zigzags, while Whitehorn balances motionless in the middle of the road. Both are giggling helplessly, which rises to shrieks of laughter as Barclay finds herself heading straight for Whitehorn. Unless Whitehorn moves, Barclay must put a foot down and concede the race. At the last possible second, Whitehorn pedals forward and crosses the finish line, and Barclay, the victor, throws her hands theatrically into the air.

This mixture of competition and playfulness perfectly sums up the cycling club. Velociposse's members are a cheerful bunch of women, trans and nonbinary people, who seem not to take themselves too seriously.

"They keep the pressure low," explains Lauryn Yuen, who has turned up on a mint-green road bike with matching bag and bottles. She tells me she has only been involved with Velociposse for a year, having taken up cycling during lockdown. She looked for a club to join when she wanted to improve her navigation ("Google Maps tries to send you onto motorways"), but the first one she tried didn't go so well. "I was the slowest, and they had to babysit me."

Behind her on Northwall Road, the rest of the group is riding in and out of a line of water bottles, chatting as they pass each other. Then, under Barclay's instruction, they pair off and attempt to do the same side by side, then with hands on each other's shoulders, then, in some cases, with their arms around each other. The giggling has not yet stopped.

This is Velociposse's Slow Skills session, which takes place once a week and is designed to improve bike handling, cornering and coordination. It also functions as a taster, with novice cyclists encouraged to join in to find out if the club is the right

fit for them. Judging from the enthusiasm of this evening's group, it has been a roaring success. The atmosphere is less that of a training session and more reminiscent of a group of preteens, hanging out on their bikes, egging each other on to do tricks, and making the most of every minute before their parents call them in for dinner.

Although most of the group are wearing Velociposse's distinctive black-and-pink garb, there is no such uniformity among their bikes. Alyssa Vongapai is on a gravel bike with large knobbly tires. Ayo Oluyemi's is a vintage steel frame with a luggage rack and downtube gear shifters. Yuen's mint-green beauty is an electric bike. Whitehorn, Velociposse's bike officer, has turned up with two. They explain that one is from a fleet of track bikes, donated by bicycle manufacturer Aventon a few years ago, that Velociposse lends out to their new riders. "We tend to give them to people who we see are going to really get into it," she says.

This seems to happen quite a lot with Velociposse. Nic Grant is relatively new to the club, having been enthusiastically recruited by another member when they attended a BMX session at the Olympic Park. Since joining they have taken up gravel riding and gone on a three-day bikepacking trip with other members of the club.

"I never imagined I could have done that," they say, describing how eagerly their clubmates lent them camping equipment, and the buzz of riding as part of a crew. "There's a big queer community within the club," they continue, explaining how Velociposse helped them as they came to terms with their gender identity.

"When I went to Slow Skills, early on, everyone was giving their pronouns. And I

(previous)   Velociposse members (left to right, top to bottom) Hayley Whitehorn, Megan Barclay, Nic Grant, Lauryn Yuen, Ayo Oluyemi, Alyssa Vongapai.
(left)   Oluyemi wearing the distinctive Velociposse jersey, with one of the track bikes donated by bicycle manufacturer Aventon.

kind of knew [I was nonbinary], but I hadn't really . . . been there. And it was a non-thing— everyone was just like, 'Here's my pronouns' and moved on. That was really nice."

Velociposse was originally conceived in 2015 as a track racing team. Then in 2017, it was relaunched as a multidisciplinary club, with a focus on widening participation. Racing nonetheless remains a big part of the group's identity.

Velociposse's website states that "there's no pressure to race, but lots of encouragement if you're up for it." The experience of Feodora Rayner, who joined the club in 2019, bears this out. Like many members, she started with the Slow Skills sessions and initially just enjoyed improving her bike handling in the company of like-minded people, without feeling any pressure to be good at it. She declined the offer of one of the Aventon track bikes, not wanting to become one of the Lycra-clad hooligans she'd seen storming through London on her commute.

But eventually she was swayed by the fervor of Thea Smith, the club's head coach and development officer, and attended a session at Herne Hill Velodrome in south London.[1] To her surprise, she enjoyed herself and discovered an underlying talent. This year she raced alongside elite international athletes at the South London Grand Prix. In October, she and teammate Sheona Arnold took part at the Masters Track World Championships in Manchester.

Rayner was briefly part of a different racing team and found the competitive atmosphere so off-putting that she considered giving up cycling altogether. Velociposse, in whose colors she now races, embraces competitiveness without putting its riders under pressure, or compromising their love of what they do. Rayner now races, not just for results, but because she genuinely loves it.

"It's not like I win everything." She laughs. "Well, sometimes I do. But I'd rather have a really fun race, where I got to try lots of things and I crossed the line fifth, than it be really boring and I just sprint past everyone."

Her enthusiasm is identical to that of the Slow Skills riders on Northwall Road. Velociposse has created a cycling community where riders of all abilities and ambition are welcomed in. They stay simply because they are having the time of their lives.

> "It was a non-thing— everyone was just like, 'Here's my pronouns' and moved on."

(1) Velociposse hosts events at Herne Hill Velodrome, such as the fixed-gear criterium, which sees riders negotiate a challenging course on bikes with just one gear. Unlike most races in the UK, riders are free to choose which gender-inclusive race category is most appropriate for them.

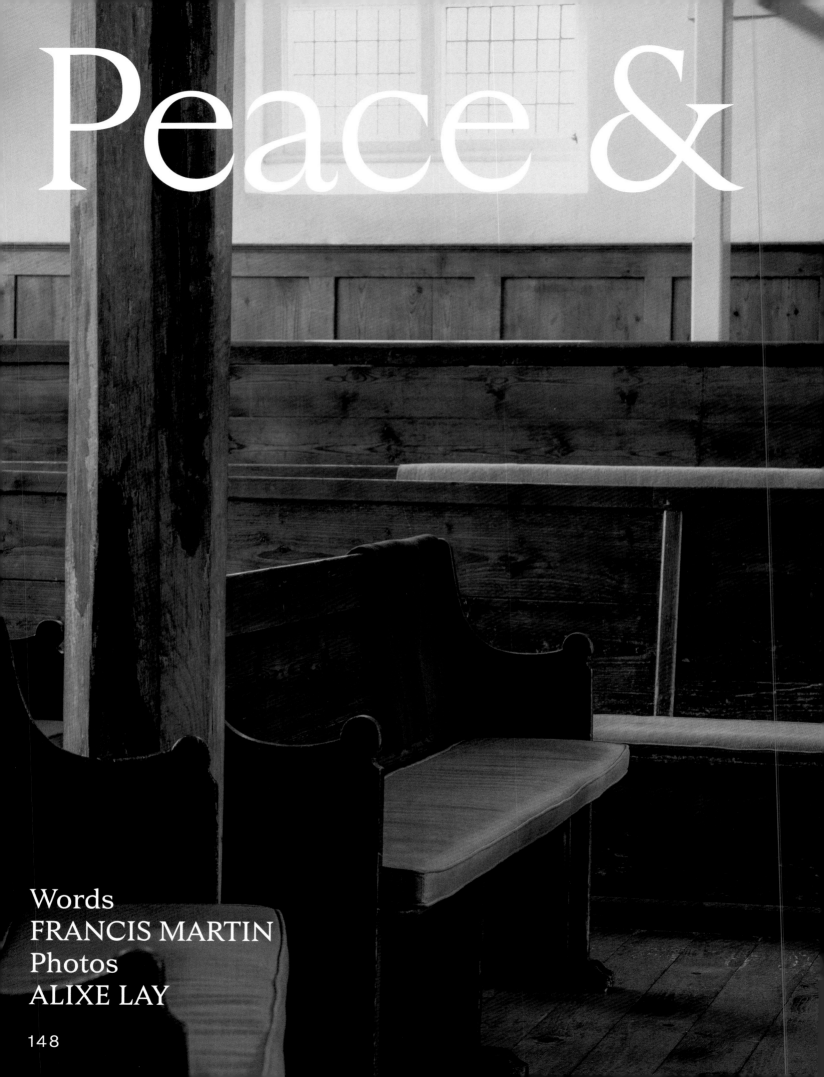

Peace &

Words
FRANCIS MARTIN
Photos
ALIXE LAY

QUIET.

In the UK, a centuries-old Quaker meeting house encourages quiet reflection.

In the absence of any other sounds, the ticking clock fills the hall. The windows are set high in the whitewashed walls, in order to prevent worshippers from being distracted. It's an old building, with faded beams and leaded windows, but its simplicity belies its age—the retrofitted metal girders that brace the walls and ceiling are the only indicator that the building is starting to feel its 350 years.

The Friends Meeting House in Hertford, 20 miles north of London, is the oldest Quaker place of worship in continuous use. It was built in 1670, little more than two decades after the movement was born in the ruins of the English Civil War. The Religious Society of Friends—better known by the sneering insult, the "Quakers"—was part of an upsurge in nonconformist Christian movements around the period when England was a republic.[1]

Most of the Quakers who funded the construction of the Hertford Meeting House were in jail at the time it was built, and a law was passed making it illegal for four or more people to gather for worship that wasn't under the auspices of the Church of England. Three and a half centuries on—and despite a significant decline in the number of British people who describe themselves as Christian—the regular attendance at the Hertford Meeting House on a Sunday morning averages 12: comfortably above that onetime legal threshold.[2]

The members gather in silence and sit for an hour, the only sound that of the ticking clock and the occasional disturbance from outside: the passage of a particularly loud motorbike on the road that runs parallel, or the wine bar next door emptying the garbage cans. "There's no minister in charge,

as Quakers believe there's something of God in everyone," explains Ruth Rankin, a Quaker who has attended the Hertford Meeting for almost 20 years. At any point in the meeting, if so moved, you may stand and contribute a reflection, though you are encouraged to only do so after sober contemplation.

(above)
The garden of the Friends Meeting House in Hertford, the oldest purpose-built Quaker meeting house still in use.

Quakerism began as an egalitarian riposte to the hierarchies of an established church in which only priests were permitted to preach. For the Quakers, personal reflection was more important than pronouncements from a pulpit, and sitting in silence was supposed to allow a more direct communication with God via the "Inner Light" that resides in each one of us. The appeal of this message has proven to be universal:

figures from 2017 suggest that there are active Quaker meetings in 87 countries across four continents, with a total of around 400,000 regular attendees. The United Kingdom, where the movement began, has around 20,000 Quakers, less than a quarter of the 121,000 who attend in Kenya, and only just fewer than Bolivia, where there are around 21,000 active Friends.

While the historical foundations of Quakerism are unambiguously Christian, and copies of the Bible lie on a small table in the center of the Hertford Meeting House, there is a strong tradition of non-Christian, and even nontheistic, Quakerism. "Not all Quakers are Christians, and they may follow different religions. Nobody's going to interrogate you," Rankin says. "There's no creed as such, which is part of why I really like coming here: Nobody's telling you what to think, what to believe. You don't have to recite things you don't believe in."

Pauline Esson has also attended meetings in Hertford for decades, but neither she nor Rankin are formally members of the Religious Society of Friends in Britain. Wariness of being categorized is a trait that many Quakers seem to share, and which the structure—or rather, lack of structure—enables. With little in the way of creed or doctrine to bind them, it might seem that a group of Quakers is merely a collection of individuals, focused on introspection rather than companionship. But the practice of shared silence itself seems to engender a strong sense of community. The English essayist Charles Lamb noticed this when he stood within the walls of the Hertford Meeting

(previous)
The interior of the Hertford Meeting House. Seating in Quaker meeting houses are always arranged so Friends face one another.

(overleaf)
The interior of the Friends Meeting House in Aylesbury, which was built in 1726.

COMMUNITY

House in the early 19th century and held the silence that stretches through the centuries. After visiting, Lamb wrote a short reflection on Quaker spirituality, included in his *Essays of Elia*, that explores the juxtaposition of silence and companionship. Two hundred years later, Esson's experience of the meeting house seems comparable. "There's something visceral that happens to me when I come in here," she says. "It's steeped in the energy that comes from people sitting together in worshipful silence. It's in the walls."

Alistair Fuller, who works in outreach for the Religious Society of Friends in Britain, suggests that the sharing of silence is intrinsic to Quakerism's open approach to belief systems. "There's a real spectrum of understanding about what we mean when we talk about the divine," he says, "but what I think undergirds all of it is a sense that what we're connecting with is beyond anyone's words, and a sense that the more we try and use words, the less helpful it is."

Fuller, like many Friends, was involved with Anglicanism before gravitating toward Quakerism. Leasa Lambert is another who arrived at Quakerism from the Church of England, but has also been part of a Baptist church and has "dabbled" with Taoism and Buddhism. She still practices Buddhism, saying that it "complements" her Quakerism.

"Even though we're sitting in silence, there is a kind of connection, there is a kind of energy from that silence, which transcends communication," Lambert says. "For me, it helps build a strong sense of community." The focus on practice, rather than belief, is redolent of certain Eastern spiritual traditions, but also brings to mind the work of sociologist Grace Davie, who has charted a tendency among European religions to attract people who "believe without belonging." For Quakers, it seems that the opposite is true—that many belong without believing the same as each other—and it appears to be a large part of the attraction.

Leilani Rabemananjara got involved with Quakerism shortly before the pandemic, when she was in her late 20s, and is now a trustee of the Young Friends General Meeting. "I was looking for a sense of community, but also the spiritual side as well," she says. "I was initially interested in the activist side: I think I just googled 'community activism.'"

While there might be, as Rabemananjara suggests, a tendency for younger Quakers to have a less overtly Christian approach, this is by no means always related to age: Martin Wright, who is in his 80s, says he is "ambivalent about the faith side," and more concerned with social action, commitment to which is a strong feature of the Quaker movement.[3]

During a meeting for worship in Brixton, south London, Wright stood and made some remarks about the need to ensure humane conditions in prison, noting that the housing project within which the meeting house stands is just a five-minute walk from Brixton Prison. In the notices after the meeting, those gathered were invited to join a silent demonstration outside an upcoming arms fair.

The meeting house in Brixton, like its counterpart in Hertford, is a purpose-built space, albeit about three centuries younger. Looking out of the window from the room where meetings for worship are held, all one can see is green: the languid tendrils of a willow tree, a hedge and some plants. It's possible to forget that we're in a housing project made up of eight-story buildings. The building is also well-used by the local community, including support groups and a poetry club.

COVID-19 lockdowns sent Quaker meetings, along with most of the rest of life, into cyberspace, and many gatherings remain partly online. In Brixton, in addition to the 13 people in the room, there were a number of attendees on Zoom on a screen to one side. Some seemed to dip in and out, most had their camera off and all were muted. At the end of the meeting, an attempt was made to join the virtual and the in-person groups for the delivery of some notices, but the microphone was out of battery and the Zoom attendees had to be jettisoned.

" Even though we're sitting in silence, there's a kind of connection—a kind of energy."

Fuller admits to some ambivalence about the role that Zoom continues to play. On the one hand, it allows greater accessibility and can be a valuable tool for outreach, as coming in person to a Quaker meeting house can, for some, be a daunting experience. It has also encouraged the building of geographically dispersed Quaker communities, highlighted by an online gathering that he attends every Wednesday for Friends across the world.

On the other hand, Fuller recognizes how valuable it is for community-building for Quakers to physically sit together and share a soundscape. For him, the extraneous noise, both from inside and outside the room, is "part of the fabric, the warp and weave of human connectedness." Sitting together and paying attention to these sounds can be a far more intimate experience than singing or reciting in unison, but when some, or all, attendees are on Zoom, with their microphones muted, the soundscape is no longer fully shared; the silence becomes siloed.

Any practical decisions that need to be made, such as whether to run hybrid meetings, are brought to a "meeting for worship for business." "The aim is to discern God's will, the natural flow of things," Rankin explains, mixing religious and spiritual language in a way that seems intuitive to many Quakers. Discernment can take some time: Voices must be heard, and action can only occur when agreement has been reached—this doesn't mean that every single person thinks it is the right decision, but that everyone acknowledges that the process has been followed.

Despite having access to these methods for reaching consensus, and the Quaker movement's long association with peace advocacy, the Hertford Meeting is riven by an intractable dispute: Some love, and others hate, the sound of the ticking clock. Rankin and Esson stand on opposite sides of the debate, but Esson concedes that, at the moment, it seems unlikely that it will be silenced, as for many it provides a useful focal point, and helps to distract from incidental sounds that invade the silence.

Alongside activism and an open-minded approach to spirituality, it is the appreciation of shared silence that seems to be the strongest glue within Quaker communities. It is, increasingly, a rare and precious thing; as Rankin puts it: "How often in your daily life do you get to sit down with a group of people and just be still?"

(1) George Fox, the movement's early leader, was tried for blasphemy in 1650. He reportedly told the magistrates to "tremble at the word of the Lord," to which one of the magistrates replied that the only quaker in court was Fox.
(2) Quakerism spread to North America in the 17th century. Despite the persecution Quakers first experienced there, today there are around 80,000 Friends in the US.
(3) Quakers have had an outsize effect on society, especially in the UK, leading humanitarian efforts like the abolition of slavery, prison reform and social justice. They were awarded the Nobel Peace Price in 1947.

FRAMA

The creative company where community is more than just a mood board.

Words
EMILY NATHAN
Photos
PAW GISSEL

(above)   Jasmin Piercy, FRAMA's finance planner, on the company's canoeing trip.

162   COMMUNITY

It's a gray Copenhagen day in August and Niels Strøyer Christophersen, the Danish founder and creative director of design brand FRAMA, is organizing sleeping bags in a newly acquired space next to his flagship showroom. There is no furniture yet, only potted plants thriving on sun-flooded windowsills and tidy piles of equipment on the floor. Plastic boxes of classic campfire foods—hot dog condiments, marshmallows for s'mores—are lined up against the walls, and new sets of cooking gear sit in neat stacks atop an army-green legion of Yeti coolers.

"I'm taking the team on a canoe trip this afternoon, to a beautiful stream I used to go to as a kid," Christophersen says, tucking a strand of hair behind his ear. "There are 26 of us going. Of course, everybody knows each other from work, but people don't really talk in the office. When you travel together like this, it's more casual; in that dead space of just getting from one place to another, people relax, and then real conversations can happen."

Christophersen speaks softly and takes up little space, but his mild manner belies a quiet confidence. Since launching FRAMA in 2011, he has guided its evolution into a sprawling, social, multidisciplinary venture that joins furniture and lighting design with accessories and self-care products, creates bespoke interior projects for clients around the world, publishes books and organizes community initiatives, from culinary experiences to art installations and events.[1]

When describing his professional trajectory, he references American media mogul David Geffen, who, as a young record executive, signed Joni Mitchell and Bob Dylan.[2] Like Geffen, he says, he too had trouble finding direction until he recognized his ability to connect the right people, and to produce something notable by enabling those relationships. The network of talent he has brought together in FRAMA—some as employees, others as collaborators—has continuously evolved to encompass ever broader and more varied disciplines. Many of these people, from designers to chefs,

pinpoint the start of their partnership with FRAMA to a casual conversation at a dinner party or a sidewalk run-in. Unusually, though, their connection to the brand often endures, even after their collaboration is complete.

"From the beginning, FRAMA was about creating real relationships that were instinctive, not strategic," says Cassandra Bradfield, an American-born designer who started as an intern at FRAMA and spent the next eight years helping to grow the fledgling company. With Christophersen's encouragement, her involvement in the brand encompassed a wide range of roles and responsibilities, from marketing and operations to design; in some ways, FRAMA "grew up" in lockstep with her own professional development.

"Niels prefers to work with people who are doing interesting things in the community, and he always allows a lot of creative freedom, which means he gives people a lot of trust," she adds. "I've shared so much of my own DNA into that brand, so I'm happy to see it succeed. Whatever forms it's taking in the years to come, whether we work together or not, I feel a lot of pride and even ownership, in a way."

The first FRAMA collection, produced in collaboration with independent designers, was a range of furniture and accessories— basic, straightforward, everyday kinds of things "with a twist." Many are now considered to be FRAMA classics: the Rivet Chair by Jonas Trampedach, its smooth aluminum sheets hammered into geometric planes; the Sintra Table, a round marble top that fits over a spherical cork base; and the Otto line of elegant, simple ceramics: clean silhouettes in matte-white stoneware. From the beginning, Christophersen let his collaborators contribute their own vision to FRAMA rather than requiring them to fit it into a prescriptive model; it is perhaps this inclusive quality that has produced such loyalty.

"Most people at FRAMA stick around," Christophersen says. "They're not just creative themselves, which is a given, but they always have something going on on the side, officially or unofficially. They have something to express, I would say, a kind of entrepreneurial soul."

Back in 2013, as the brand was finding its footing in a workshop in Copenhagen's outlying Nordhavn district, Christophersen realized that it was being described—by visitors, by designers, by the press—as "industrial." Having a label, any label, assigned to FRAMA was antithetical to Christophersen's intentions, but it forced him to understand that the space in which his brand was presented had a significant impact on how it was experienced. He set out to find a home for FRAMA that would express its values without limiting it, and his search led him to a 19th-century apothecary nestled among the quaint row houses of the Nyboder neighborhood in the city center.

St. Paul's Apothecary seemed a strange choice for FRAMA, at first. Elaborate wooden cornices, a complex network of oak pharmaceutical cabinets and an ornately painted ceiling contributed to an elaborate, baroque atmosphere that was quite the opposite of FRAMA's material-forward, essentialist aesthetic. But Christophersen saw the possibilities that others did not.

FRAMA's new space was pivotal in enabling the brand to expand both its offerings and its activities, and to connect more conveniently with Copenhagen's creative community. It was at this essential juncture, for example, that Christophersen met Danish perfumer Lena Norling. "One day, we were discussing how we could encapsulate the brand in a different way," Norling remembers. "[It's] one thing that someone sits on a FRAMA stool, but how can we bring the feeling of the brand closer to people? I proposed making a scent inspired by the beautiful old pharmacy and FRAMA's place inside it."

The perfume kick-started the development of the St Paul's Apothecary Collection, which has since introduced numerous perfumes and self-care products. Soon to follow was the inauguration of the "long-table gathering," a quarterly culinary experience held in the shop with former Noma chef Mikkel Karstad. Bridging the gap between FRAMA products in the showroom and in real life—offering them up to people as plates to be eaten from and tables to be dined at—was the next step in aligning the business with a cohesive, holistic lifestyle.

"From the toothbrush we choose to our chair or bike, where we travel or what we eat or where we shop—these are choices, and there's a clear pattern," Christophersen says. "I believe everything in our lives is connected, curated, even without intention, and I think that simple fact can create a sense of community."

Today, FRAMA encompasses a collection of intersecting "spheres"—the Permanent Collection of furniture, the Studio Collection of kitchen cabinets and bathroom units, the St Paul's Apothecary Collection of self-care products and fragrances, the Studio Store in Copenhagen, and the architectural practice—and there is always room for another collaboration.[3]

"When a creative person decides to work with someone, it's usually because there is a sense that you speak the same language," Norling says. "Niels is good at finding people. He starts with a feeling that this person can translate their vision into FRAMA— and then he simply allows them to do that."

As for the canoe trip, good food was cooked over open flames, and connections were made off the grid. The tents, it turned out, weren't quite waterproof enough for the particularly rainy Danish summer. Everybody woke up wet, but nobody seemed to mind.

(1) Among FRAMA's notable interior design projects is an apartment and studio in a 15th-century villa outside Florence for the Spanish film director Albert Moya.
(2) Geffen would go on to create film studio DreamWorks Pictures with Steven Spielberg and Jeffrey Katzenberg. In 2023, he was estimated by Forbes to have a net worth of $7.7 billion.
(3) The Copenhagen store is also home to APOTEK 57, a bakery and cafe run by chef Chiara Barla.

" Most people at FRAMA stick around."

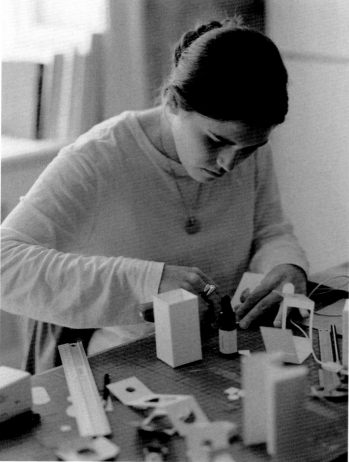

(left)
Teodora Kolchagova, FRAMA's
head of PR and communications
(top) and Anna Duran (bottom), a
junior spatial planner.

(opposite)
The FRAMA studio store in
central Copenhagen.

COMMUNITY

The art and
agriculture collective sowing
seeds of community.

New ROOTS.

A grapevine twists through a pergola in the hills above Battir, an ancient Palestinian village just west of Bethlehem. Clusters of grapes dangle over a tranquil, shaded terrace that looks out on an ancient scene—terraces of dry stone walls, olive groves and Roman-era irrigation systems. The landscape is a living history: In 2014, Battir was awarded UNESCO World Heritage Site status in honor of the traditional agricultural methods still practiced there.[1]

Farther down the valley, however, is a poignant symbol of more recent history—a barbed wire fence separating the occupied West Bank from Jerusalem.[2] The Israeli military often prevents Palestinian farmers in Gaza and the West Bank from accessing their land during harvest on the pretext of security concerns, and in recent years, Israeli settlers have routinely burned fields and cut down olive and fruit trees to try and eradicate Palestinians from their lands. According to data gathered by the UN, 5,000 olive trees were vandalized in Palestinian West Bank villages in less than five months in 2023 alone.

"Every day, we're losing more varieties of grapevines—along with the land," says Vivien Sansour, who runs the Palestine Heirloom Seed Library from a 300-square-foot room adjacent to the terrace. Sansour, an artist and conservationist, speaks of the grape harvest as a symbol of Palestinian unity and social solidarity, a throwback to a time when baskets laden with produce traveled neighbor to neighbor.

For Sansour, the ritual of the harvest demonstrates a shared kinship and the community's resilience; a tradition of giving and receiving. "You did not need to have everything to actually have everything," she says, remembering a time when people produced and shared their food within the community.

"Diversity was the responsibility of the collective—diversity on the plate, diversity of skills, and the respect of living by season," she says, explaining that Palestinian culture is shaped by this seasonal approach to food. "Palestinians' traditional experience with the land is like the experiences of most Indigenous cultures around the world: a communal relationship with everything around us."

It's a spirit Sansour seeks to preserve and renew more broadly through the Seed Library, where, since 2014, she and a collective of colleagues and farmers have been recovering and safeguarding a trove of seeds native to Palestine.[3] The library operates a seed swap—farmers are given native seeds that they grow without using chemicals, and at the end of the season, they return the same number of seeds to the library. Typically, groups of young Palestinians will help older farmers with harvesting their crops and cleaning the fields.

Sansour's vision for the project is deeply rooted in her upbringing on another sun-kissed hillside just beyond Bethlehem—once a tranquil and rustic landscape, adorned with orchards of fruit and olives, that has since been extensively built-up.

"When we lose olive trees, we're losing beautiful concepts in Palestine like al Ouneh, which is when the community lends a hand to anyone doing a big task, like harvesting olives, because there's an understanding and humility about our human condition which is that we need each other to survive," says Sansour.

Sansour is concerned about becoming reliant on buying seeds from Israel, and the chemical intervention that is required to grow them. Like most farmers around the world, those in Palestine are beholden to modern agribusiness and international seed corporations. Heirloom seeds, like those collected by the seed bank, are non-genetically modified and naturally pollinated, and offer an alternative to a system that requires farmers to purchase new seeds and chemicals every year.

(1) Battir was listed as a World Heritage Site after an emergency nomination from the Palestinian National Authority. The committee recognized that: "The agricultural practices that were used to create this living landscape reflect one of the oldest farming methods known to humankind and are an important source of livelihood for local communities."

(2) The Israeli West Bank Barrier had been planned to pass through Battir. In 2007, the village sued Israel's Defense Ministry to alter the course of the wall, and its route was also opposed by the Israel Nature and Parks Authority—the first time an Israeli government agency had opposed the route of the wall.

(3) The heirloom seeds collected by the library include bitinjan, a type of eggplant, sabanikh, a type of spinach and the Jadu'I watermelon, which Sansour spent six years searching for. She eventually found the seeds in a drawer in a local farmer's house, next to his nuts and bolts.

Words
VERA SAJRAWI
Photos
SAMAR HAZBOUN &
MAX HEMPHILL

> " Community for me is where everybody can have the space and liberty to be who they are."

Fatima Muammer, a Palestinian woman, tends to the library daily. She orchestrates the seed swap with a network of farmers in Battir. "I love what I do and I love how happy farmers are when they work with us," says Muammer. "Some seeds are hard to find and when farmers see [that they are] available here, they become very excited and flood us with information on how to plant and preserve them."[4] It's a form of knowledge that extends beyond science to centuries-old rituals like the feast of Saint George's Day, where the act of planting is celebrated by sowing seeds, sharing picnics and making offerings of olive oil at the local churches.

Sansour says that Palestinians need *al Ouneh* now more than ever before. "The Palestine I love and fight for is the Palestine that lives and breathes a culture of communion and respect with all living beings." She hopes initiatives like the seed bank will give farmers in Palestine and around the world the freedom to be self-reliant and independent from large corporations. "I want them to have the willingness to imagine that a different reality is possible."

She continues, "Community for me is where everybody can have the space and liberty to be who they are, a space that values the full cycle of life—a safe space where you can live safely and die safely."

(4) The seeds are also available for visitors to purchase at the library and are sold online through Disarming Design from Palestine.

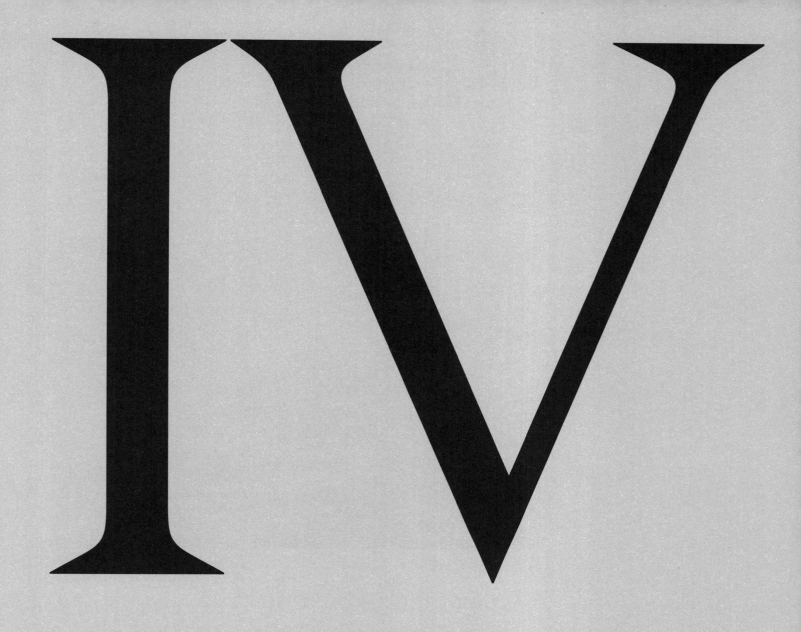

IV

DIRECTORY
A guide to the season.

FIELD NOTES

Words:
Jessica J. Lee

A new nature column.

It is midwinter at Alexanderplatz station in Berlin. A single starling hops along the platform, between the McDonald's wrappers and empty beer bottles. Suddenly, it lifts off—black wings glinting blue and green—to join hundreds of its kind dancing against the pink evening sky.

A murmuration of starlings is one of the great joys of winter. This spectacle of collective movement can feature anything from a few hundred to hundreds of thousands of birds, all whirling with liquid synchronicity. As bird-watcher and author Tim Dee writes in *The Running Sky*, it resembles "iron filings made to bend to a magnet," each bird closely monitoring the flight of its neighbors and reacting in milliseconds to tiny changes in direction. For the starlings, these gatherings have a practical purpose: They offer safety in numbers and a chance to exchange information on where to find food—a ritual gathering before turning in for a night of rest.

From October to March, Scandinavian starling populations can be seen gathering throughout the UK and continental Europe, with some groups migrating as far as the Iberian Peninsula and northern Africa. In North America—where starlings are considered an invasive species, having been introduced in the late 19th century—the birds migrate as far south as northern Mexico. But in Europe, where there are temperate winters, they often hang around; with their numbers declining due to modern agriculture and habitat loss, the sight of a murmuration feels especially poignant.

Catching their show is simply a matter of planning: Opt for clear, cool weather, and keep an eye out an hour before sunset. Starlings gather near woodlands, in suburban shrubs, near wild cliffs, lakes, rivers, and even buildings—just about anywhere they can find good shelter. If you want to improve your odds, choose a spot they're known to dance: Night after night, swimmers and beachgoers gather to appreciate the acrobatics overhead near Brighton Pier in the UK; across the Atlantic, New York's Central Park is a frequent haunt for starlings. Dress warmly, find a clearing and look skyward.

Words:
Alice Vincent

Our seasonal guide to gardening.

Winter can be tough for gardeners. The short days and miserable weather often feel like something to endure rather than enjoy: a time to prune plants, tidy up sheds and wait for spring to return.

Even seasoned horticulturalists hunker down in winter, and it's understandable if those less green-fingered assume their garden is just lying dormant in the colder months. Yet winter is a crucial, if blunt, season. Nothing can bloom year-round and most perennial plants will hibernate beneath the earth, gathering energy for the long days ahead. Some, however, take advantage of the quietude of winter to unearth themselves, blooming in the dimmer days. Of these, the hellebores are perhaps the most reliable and delightful.

Hellebores—or Christmas or Lenten roses, as they are more commonly known—are winter stalwarts. Resolutely low-maintenance and tolerant of shade, they make excellent plants for urban gardens and busy beginners, blooming from midwinter all the way through to April or May. Their elegant, nodding flowerheads can vary from crisp white to vivid pinks and purples, and they are botanically promiscuous, leading to new combinations of colors—especially in the "freckles" spotted inside the petals.

Some practical advice: While they can survive for a couple of years in a container, hellebores will flourish better in the ground. If you don't have access to a garden, consider passing them along to someone who does once they've gone to seed in the spring.[1] They enjoy damp, low-light conditions but won't thrive in waterlogged soil, so water sparingly if your plants don't have direct access to rainfall. Hellebores are also notoriously feeble in the vase: Slice through the bottom third of the stems with a sharp knife if you're cutting them for the house.

Over the centuries, folklore has associated hellebores with both delirium and reassurance; you may find that they evoke both feelings when they first appear, radiant against the soggy winter soil.

(1) A normal part of the life cycle of many plants, going to seed is the stage at which a plant is no longer flowering or producing fruit and is directing its energy to producing seeds.

Writer HUA HSU on faxes and friendship.

New Yorker staff writer Hua Hsu began writing his Pulitzer Prize–winning memoir *Stay True* 25 years ago, even if he didn't realize it at the time. "It wasn't writing that I necessarily thought would become a book someday," says Hsu. He started recording his thoughts the night he heard that his best friend, Ken, had been murdered in a senseless act of violence while the pair were college students at the University of California, Berkeley. "It was just my own method of coping."

Stay True is a beautiful tribute to a formative friendship and led Hsu in surprising directions. "It was very unexpected to end up in a place that felt far more hopeful than I thought would be possible when I set out to write back in 1998," Hsu says on a video call from upstate New York. There were other surprises too. While the memoir's title is inspired by a phrase that Ken would often say, Hsu noticed it cropping up repeatedly—in daily conversation, song titles and lyrics. "It's a title that continues to unfold for me in different ways," he says.

SUYIN HAYNES: In *Stay True*, you include photographs and scans of old flyers, as well as excerpts from faxes your father sent to you when you were growing up in the US and he was in Taiwan. Do you still have the hard copies at home?

HUA HSU: I definitely still have hard copies of all the faxes. I am the type of person who holds on to everything and then spends a lot of time thinking about who I was when I first held these things.
SH: How important was it to you to include these different ways of communicating in the book?

HH: I think of it as if you're walking down a hallway and you peek into different people's dorm rooms. You get a sense of who they are, but you don't really get the full story. It was important [for that reason] that we didn't caption or belabor the images.
SH: How did you strike a balance between sharing your experience and keeping certain parts of yourself private?

HH: There's a version of the book that's probably twice as long where I kept everything in. I was very happy to edit it down. I felt like it made more sense for it to be a shorter book, but I also just like the idea of keeping certain things to myself.
SH: You include musings on friendship from philosophers like Aristotle and Jacques Derrida. What's your own philosophy on the subject?

HH: I don't think I have one. When I was younger, my approach to friendship was that someone should complete me. Thinking about my friendship with Ken, and about him as an absence as I grew older, I realized that that's just one part of friendship. Part of it is also leaving yourself open to who you might become and allowing yourself to be understood and to understand someone else.
SH: You write: "Sifting through these small moments of the past was a way of resisting the future." Has the process of writing *Stay True* changed the way you think about the future?

HH: My relationship with this loss was to try and tunnel my way back to the past. I think that that's a natural response to loss. You want to return to some kind of halcyon moment where things haven't fallen apart. But that makes it much harder to look to the future, to look forward, because you feel as though you're abandoning the past, you feel as though you're abandoning this memory. And I realized while writing the book that you could do both of these things: that you could be happy and sad at the same time, that you could mourn someone but also celebrate them.
SH: At *The New Yorker*, you write cultural criticism and profiles, and explore Asian American history. What's the commonality among the stories you're drawn to?

HH: I'm interested in how people imagine the future, and what people are capable of imagining. Whether it's music or politics, I'm always interested in why someone sees the horizon they see, and what compelled them to see that as opposed to something else.
SH: What does "staying true" mean to you?

HH: As I've lived alongside the book, I've realized that we [will often] have a fantasy that there's this true version of ourselves and we just need to get there, that it's on the horizon, and that we will someday become the person we want to become. But there's no definitive horizon for a lot of us. It's just about staying true to who you might become, or who you could become. That's the important part.

(1) *Stay True* also won the 2022 National Book Critics Circle award in autobiography and was described by *New York Magazine* as "an evolutionary step for Asian American literature."

COMING TOGETHER

Crossword: Mark Halpin

ACROSS

1. Butters from India
6. "Now!"
10. Obscure or cover
14. Way to get somewhere
15. Mambo King Puente
16. Brute
17. City-related
18. Free of debt or responsibility
20. Group of edifice enthusiasts?
22. Berlin to Sarajevo dir.
23. Cries in a corrida
24. First name in soul
28. Conditions
29. Useful "Wheel of Fortune" purchase, often
30. One of 24 in your body
31. Group of fans of a certain type of orange juice?
36. De Armas of "Knives Out"
37. Where the majority of humans live
38. Divest (of)
39. Ultimate goals
40. Cooking spray brand
41. Group of rodent aficionados?
45. Self-centeredness
46. Total
47. Juvenile
48. Make even more fine, perhaps
50. Widdle or Waruk, in the Star Wars universe
52. "Ewww, stop telling me that!"
55. Group of guitarist Bo's devotees?
58. Graph shape showing normal distribution
61. Tom who played Mozart in "Amadeus"
62. Sphere
63. Characters going after bees?
64. Baryshnikov, to friends
65. Uber alternative
66. Star or Sun follower in brand names
67. "No bid from me"
—

RECEIVED WISDOM

Words:
Benjamin Dane

Marimekko's creative director, REBEKKA BAY, on leadership and finding the right work-life balance.

I was still in design school when I got my first job in fashion. I was curious about the application process and building a portfolio and mostly just for fun I applied for a job at Mr., a menswear chain in Denmark that was looking for a head of design to create their first in-house collection. I assembled a portfolio and went to my very first job interview.

Much to my surprise, I ended up getting the job. Suddenly, while only in my second year of school, I was the chief designer of a hyper-commercial menswear company.

I learned the hard way to not bite off more than you can chew. I remember crying from exhaustion after my first day trying to pick between 200 different checkered

patterns at Première Vision, a huge, international fabric trade fair in Paris. But by the time I finished design school, I'd already got an understanding of the commercial context, which most people don't do until they graduate.

I've always been fascinated by the zeitgeist; the reason why people are drawn to certain trends at certain times, like a seasonal color in fashion. When I graduated, the trend forecasting industry did not exist in Denmark, so I moved to London and got a job at a small firm. I had a boss who led by fear, but I did at least learn what type of manager I didn't want to be. Today, I believe the most important thing for a leader is to let go.[1] Give a precise brief but remember to trust in your team and the process, and try not to micromanage everything. I think of myself as a conductor whose primary responsibility is to set the tone of the orchestra.

People might be surprised to know that I don't consider myself a minimalist. I can see why people would call me that—after all, I did create COS for H&M—but I'm not very interested in minimalism as an art movement. Rather, I want to create something that is relevant for as many people as possible, and I

believe a certain amount of distillation is required in the design process.

My biggest achievement is that I have a 17-year-old son and a partner I've been happily married to for 28 years, despite working extremely long hours for almost my entire career. As time-consuming as my work is, it has never been at the expense of my family—maybe because I've always insisted that the two could coexist.

I don't have many regrets, but if I were to do something over, I would spend more time in school. When I was younger, I couldn't wait to get to work and didn't appreciate how much of a privilege it is to be able to immerse yourself completely in a subject. Before I went to design school, I studied art history—maybe I'll pick that up again someday.

(1) Bay says that she feels most relaxed when working but that when she does unwind in the traditional sense of the word, it's often through hiking or cooking. "I approach cooking in much the same way as I approach design; I try to express myself as simply as possible," she says.

TOP TIP

Words:
John Ovans

CHRISTOPHER JOHN ROGERS on mastering vibrant colors at home.

I grew up in the South and remember seeing churchgoers dressed head to toe in yellow and green, with matching shirts, ties and hats. They were never afraid to be declarative with the clothes they wore.

Something as simple as color can provoke a profound reaction in people—I've always tried to channel that in my approach to fashion, and now also in interiors. What I love about Carte Blanche—the range of paints and wallpaper patterns I recently designed for Farrow & Ball—is that I can provide tools for people to express themselves with color. If you'd like to experiment with color at home, there are some easy ways to get started. Take it one room at a time and perhaps begin with the ceiling to see how a particular color makes you feel. Remember that any room with good light can take color well, and it's a great way to liven up small spaces, like a hallway.

Don't think your only options are either an all-neutral space or a maximalist full-color box: Injecting a burst of color in a restrained way can still really enliven the space and allow your personality to shine—even if it's just a striped border at the bottom of the wall or a bright rug.

As you start to become more confident, you can experiment with analogous colors—the colors next to one another on the color wheel. I find it best to stick to a maximum of three. For example, if you're painting a wall or a room a cool blue, the trim could be in a lighter, brighter blue. You get the harmony of the two blue tones, but also a surprising element that energizes the space. It's a great way to make a room feel like it has your name on it and can help you find the right balance between being fun and out there and creating somewhere comfortable and livable.
—

Words:
Tara Joshi

Film composer EMILE MOSSERI on the art of setting music to film.

The American composer Emile Mosseri creates evocative, delicate soundscapes for film and television. In recent years that's included *Kajillionaire, The Last Black Man in San Francisco* and *Minari*, for which he received an Oscar nomination. His scores quietly stir something in the viewer, informing how we understand and interpret what we're seeing on screen. Here he reveals how the composer is an essential player in helping a director bring a story to life.

TARA JOSHI: How did you get into writing music for films?

EMILE MOSSERI: I found it as a teenager, through [composer] Danny Elfman and *Edward Scissorhands*. I fell in love with it. I fell in love with Winona Ryder, but I realized the music was doing a lot of that too—it's such an unapologetically romantic, sweeping score. It made me realize that it was a job, that people wrote this music.

I studied [film scoring] in school, but I was on tour for all of my 20s, just playing in bands. Over the years I'd worked with different people, scoring friends' films, but it wasn't until I moved to LA that I dove into it more seriously. That was about five years ago.

TJ: What's the process of writing a score?

EM: The cool thing about scoring films is that each project and director is totally different, so you have to learn as you go. You come in at the final stage of the filmmaking process, which I'm told is often the most fun part for directors; it's all coming together and it's romantic, and I feel lucky to be a part of that.[1]

Sometimes you watch the film and have conversations with the director, and then you write music and see what works. But the way I have had the most success is by writing a lot of music in the spirit of the film; either by using a rough cut of the film or a script. I'll write

themes and melodies that are inspired by the story, and then they assemble the movie with the music.

Some people write specific music for a specific scene, but for me, that feels too functional. I find I have more luck writing when I'm moved by the story, and then playing it against an unexpected scene. In that chaos, you capture something magical.

TJ: Why is music such an important part of how we watch films?

EM: After smell, music is the most powerful way to light up the receptors in your brain associated with nostalgia; and until they start pumping smells into movie theaters, music is the best way to make people feel something.

I think you have to respect that and not abuse it, because it can feel emotionally manipulative. The trick is doing it in a way that the audience doesn't feel manipulated. The music should sneak up

from behind and wash over you.

TJ: What role does silence play in writing a film score?

EM: The use of silence can be really effective and it's important to know where not to use music. I'm drawn to films where [the actors] have a unique voice, or where they're ripping their hearts out and putting them on the screen. That [vulnerability] can be more powerful if you exercise restraint with the music.

(1) While most film scores are written for specific scenes, there are few notable examples where the film is cut to fit the music. These include Ennio Morricone's scores for Sergio Leone's *Dollars Trilogy*, which he prepared months before the films' production ended, and the end of *E.T. the Extra-Terrestrial*, which director Steven Spielberg edited to fit music by John Williams.

Photos: Edvinas Bruzas

POWER TOOL

Words:
Elle Hunt

Master piano tuner ULRICH GERHARTZ on the tool he couldn't work without.

I've been with Steinway & Sons all my life. I started nearly 37 years ago as an apprentice at the factory in Hamburg, manufacturing pianos. Now I'm a concert technician, working with artists and venues to ensure that they have the right instrument in the best possible condition. I know pretty much every concert grand in the UK and Ireland, and there are a number of A-list pianists who want me with them wherever they play.

I do my job the same way as it was done a hundred years ago. There's no computer involved. I tune the piano completely by ear, using a tuning fork to get the pitch. My tool kit is huge, but this particular tool, the toning needle holder, I've had for 35 years—it was given to me as an apprentice for getting good results in my exams.

It's essentially just a handle with a way to fix three needles into it, but it has been used by piano makers for centuries. On a concert grand you have 243 strings and 88 hammers, which go from a big hammer in the bass, which will hit a string that is nearly two meters [approximately 6½ feet] long, to

a little hammer in the treble that hits a string that is about 40 millimeters [about 1½ inches] long. When preparing a concert piano, the final stage is always the voicing of the hammer heads with the toning needle holder. By changing the texture of the felt, you can precisely balance the sound of the piano and create the best tone and dynamics.

The beauty of a Steinway piano is that it is hand-built—they all have their own personality. Part of my expertise is to use this tool to unearth the personality of the piano in its raw state, and then bring that out and nurture it. There's a lot of tender loving care and preparation that goes into settling the piano before I'm confident in it. There might be one note that the pianist thinks is too bright or too mellow, but it will really be the finishing touches.

The quality and simplicity of this toning needle holder is such that it is likely to last for decades. All it needs is a steady supply of sharp needles to keep going. I am sure that eventually it will be passed on to the next generation of piano concert technicians.

CREDITS

COVER:	PHOTOGRAPHER	Edgar Berg
	ART DIRECTOR	Christian Møller Andersen
	STYLIST	Julia Quante
	MAKEUP	Paloma Brytscha
	HAIR	Noriko Takayama
	DOP	Sheldon Harris at Scusi Berlin
	PRODUCER	Franziskus Dornhege at Scusi Berlin
	PRODUCTION	Marcel Calliku
	MODELS	Azza, Hanna and Hannes at Izaio Management. Miriam, Momo and Tru at M4 Models. Idrica, John and Celine at Viva Models
		Alero at Neu Casting
	ASSISTANTS	Florina Avyas, Natasha Els, Atsushi Imai, Mai Linh Le, Michelle Parilla de la Puente, Frederik Zieher

CAROLINE POLACHEK:	PRODUCTION ASSISTANT	Savannah Meetze
	GAFFER	Gordon Yould
	ART ASSISTANT	Tara Tajdini

ANGELA TRIMBUR:	1ST ASSISTANT	Benjamin Joseph
	2ND ASSISTANT	Andrew Harless
	3RD ASSISTANT	Alexis Sotomayor
	STYLING ASSISTANTS	Cataline Bulgach, Graciela Paulina

SPECIAL THANKS:		Christian Møller Andersen
		Harriet Fitch Little
		Scusi Berlin

STOCKISTS:
A — Z

POINT OF VIEW

Words:
George Upton

Poet VICTORIA ADUKWEI BULLEY describes a scene from her local library.

I'm sitting in the gardens of Lea Bridge Library in east London. It's late summer and I'm shaded by the tall trees, looking up at an intensely blue sky. With the red brick of the library, it makes for a wonderfully colorful palette. There's a wooden climbing frame for children to climb and large rocks and plants of different heights, and from here I can see both the Victorian row houses and Lea Bridge Road, so it feels residential and urban at the same time.

Behind me is the library's new extension, a pavilion designed by Studio Weave in wood and red concrete that runs along one side of the garden. It's 11:30 a.m. and there's a stay-and-play coffee morning in session; I can see the babies crawling around through the large windows. There are a few kids playing in the garden, watched by their parents, the strollers tucked away by the entrance, but it's calm, it's not too busy.

I feel very lucky that this is my local library. For a writer, any library is a sort of sacred space, housing those things that made you the writer you are, and a home for the work that you make. But to have this public space—that is beautiful and completely free to access—when many libraries are closing across the country, is really special.

The library was one of the many hundreds in the UK funded by Andrew Carnegie, the American steel magnate, and was built in 1905. With this extension and its intentional architecture, the library feels new. I had always seen it solely as a space for work or study but then, when I became a mother, I started coming for the parent and baby mornings. After the extension was built, they invited people to help plant the garden as part of the landscaping. The day we were planting I bumped into a friend that I had met at one of those mornings and asked her to join in. I love knowing that, no matter where we live, we will be able to come here and say to our kids: "We planted that one, that's the one you did."

I was aiming to capture that sense of sharing in something at the end of my poetry collection, *Quiet*. I write about tending to the soil as the foundation of all that we live off and stand upon, and how the act of planting is a collective one. It can be hard to feel like you own anything in a big city like London—ownership in the best sense of the word, the sense of having a claim and belonging to a place. It's nice that, in a small way, I can feel that here.